Making
the Most *of*
Your Money
*in Tough
Times*

Kerby Anderson

HARVEST HOUSE PUBLISHERS
EUGENE, OREGON

Cover by Dugan Design Group, Bloomington, Minnesota

Cover photo © Image Source / Image Source Pink / Jupiterimages

This book is not intended to take the place of sound professional financial advice. Neither the author nor the publisher assumes any liability for possible adverse consequences as a result of the information contained herein.

MAKING THE MOST OF YOUR MONEY IN TOUGH TIMES
Copyright © 2009 by Kerby Anderson
Published by Harvest House Publishers
Eugene, Oregon 97402
www.harvesthousepublishers.com

Library of Congress Cataloging-in-Publication Data
    Anderson, J. Kerby.
    Making the most of your money in tough times / Kerby Anderson.
        p. cm.
    Includes bibliographical references.
    ISBN 978-0-7369-2466-5 (pbk.)
    1. Money—Biblical teaching. 2. Finance, Personal—Religious aspects—Christianity.
I. Title.
    BS680.M57A53 2009
    241'.68—dc22

                                        2009003602

Printed in the United States of America

        09 10 11 12 13 14 15 16 17 / BP-SK / 10 9 8 7 6 5 4 3 2 1

Contents

Getting Back *to* Basics

We need sound advice in tough economic times. When I started writing this book, I was predicting we would be in for some tough times. Before I finished, those tough economic times had already arrived. As I set forth in the later chapters of this book, it's possible that our current economic challenge is merely a preview of coming attractions.

A real-estate bust and banking crisis will correct themselves over time, unless government officials make the problem worse. But the long-term challenges of the federal debt, trade deficits, and unfunded liabilities are certain to have a negative impact in the future.

One clear lesson from history is that we cannot control the actions of others, but we can control our own. Sure, we can vote politicians out of office at election time, but we don't have too much control over what they do. And we have even less control over the booms and busts of an economy.

But we *can* control what *we* do. And the tough times we're experiencing right now are a good reason to get back to basics and apply biblical principles to economics and finance.

What is a biblical perspective on money and materialism? What does the Bible say about giving, saving, and spending? What can we do to get out of debt? How much insurance should we purchase? What is the future of the American economy? And what will be the impact of the global economy?

These are questions I attempt to answer so you can make the most of your money in these tough times. We need to apply biblical principles to our own finances and then call our elected officials to apply those principles to the economy. Reading this book is the first step in learning how to apply them.

1

Money

Does the Bible have something to say about money? Actually, it says quite a bit about it. It's estimated that about 140 verses in the Bible deal with the subject of money. If you add in the other verses that talk about gold and silver (which were two forms of currency), then the number of verses exceeds 800.

In this book we'll look at what the Scriptures say about giving, saving, spending, debt, and credit. We'll provide practical suggestions for how to save money, how to buy insurance, and how to invest. And we'll answer many of the most-asked questions concerning money and finances.

What does the Bible say about money?

We should start by correcting a common cliché—that money is the root of all evil. Actually, the biblical passage says,

> The love of money is a root of all kinds of evil, for which some have strayed from the faith in their greediness, and pierced themselves through with many sorrows (1 Timothy 6:10 NKJV).

So it's not money that is evil, but the *love* of money that is the concern. Money can be used to promote good or evil. Money can provide for your family, feed the poor, and promote the gospel. It can also be used to buy drugs, engage in prostitution, and destroy individuals and society.

The real question is, What's your attitude toward money? What do you plan to do with the financial resources God has placed into your hands? Jesus warned us that we shouldn't love money, because we can't serve both God and Mammon—wealth (see Matthew 6:24). In order to have a proper biblical perspective on money, we first need to understand what the Bible teaches about wealth and poverty.

A biblical view of wealth

Our materialistic culture and consumer-oriented society have been seducing Christians into an economic lifestyle that does not glorify God. Some have adopted a materialistic lifestyle, while others have tried to live a counterculture lifestyle.

Even within the Christian community, believers are bombarded with unbiblical views of wealth. At one extreme are those who preach a prosperity gospel of "health and wealth" for all believers. At the other extreme are radicals who condemn all wealth and imply that a rich Christian is a contradiction in terms.

What is a biblical view of wealth? At first glance, the Bible seems to teach that wealth is wrong for Christians. It appears to even condemn the wealthy. After all, both Jesus and the Old Testament prophets preached against materialism and seemed to say at times that true believers cannot possess wealth. If this is so, then all of us in Western society are in trouble, because we are all wealthy by New Testament standards.

But a comprehensive look at the relevant biblical passages quickly reveals that a biblical view of wealth is more complex. In fact, Scripture teaches three basic principles about wealth.

- First, *wealth itself is not condemned.* The Bible teaches that God gave material wealth to Abraham, Isaac, Jacob, and Joseph (see Genesis 13; 26; 30; 39 respectively). Other individuals in the Old Testament were also wealthy, such as Job (Job 42) and Solomon (1 Kings 3). In fact, we see in Job chapter 42 that God once again blessed Job with material possessions after his trials. In Deuteronomy, Proverbs, and Ecclesiastes, wealth is seen as evidence of God's blessing (see Deuteronomy 8; 28; Proverbs 22:2; Ecclesiastes 5:19).

• Second, *when wealthy people in the Bible were condemned, they were condemned for the means by which their riches were obtained,* not for the riches themselves. The Old Testament prophet Amos thundered against the injustice of obtaining wealth through oppression or fraud (5:11). Micah spoke out against the unjust scales and light weights with which Israel defrauded the poor (6:11). Neither Amos nor Micah condemned wealth per se; they only denounced the unjust means by which it is sometimes achieved.

• Third, *Christians should be concerned about the effect wealth can have on our lives.* We read in many passages that wealth often tempts us to forget about God. Proverbs 30:8-9 says, "Give me neither poverty nor riches; feed me with the food that is my portion, that I not be full and deny You and say, 'Who is the LORD?'" Hosea 13:6 says of those who were satisfied that "their heart became proud" and they ultimately forgot about the Lord.

Wealthy believers may no longer look to God for their provision because they can meet their basic needs by themselves. We read in Ecclesiastes 2 and 5 that people who are wealthy cannot really enjoy their wealth. Even billionaires often reflect on the fact that they cannot really enjoy the wealth they have. Moreover, Proverbs 28:11 and Jeremiah 9:23 warn that wealth often leads to pride and arrogance.

The tale of two rich men

The title of one of my sermons is "The Tale of Two Rich Men." It's based upon the stories of the rich young ruler (Luke 18) and Zacchaeus (Luke 19). Both were wealthy, but that's where the similarity ends.

Some have said that the rich young ruler is the only person in the Gospels who came to Jesus and went away worse than he came. He wanted to know what he should do to inherit eternal life. That was his problem: He wanted to know what to *do*. He wanted to work his way to salvation.

Jesus does not tell him to give 10 percent to the poor. The rich young ruler probably had already done that. Instead, Jesus confronts him by challenging him to give up his possessions:

> One thing you still lack; sell all that you possess and distribute it to the poor, and you shall have treasure in heaven; and come, follow Me (Luke 18:22).

It's obvious from the passage that this isn't what the rich young ruler wanted to hear, since he went away sad. Jesus then teaches that it's hard for a rich man to enter the kingdom of heaven.

Where is your trust?

Even though wealth might be an evidence of God's blessing, believers are not to trust in it. Passages in the Old Testament and the New Testament teach that the believer should not trust in wealth but in God (Proverbs 11:4,28; Jeremiah 9:23; 1 Timothy 6:17; James 1:11; 5:2).

We have a very different conclusion to the story of another rich man, by the name of Zacchaeus. Although his name means "righteous one," he was not living up to it. Tax collectors were devious people who would skim off part of the taxes for themselves. Being a tax collector was a great job for someone with no conscience.

Yet the story ends differently from that of the rich young ruler. Zacchaeus climbs a sycamore-fig tree, is called down by Jesus, and then brings Him to his house. Zacchaeus then announces, "Half of my possessions I will give to the poor, and if I have defrauded anyone of anything, I will give back four times as much" (Luke 19:8). It is worth noting that he was planning to do much more than the law required. The penalty for defrauding someone was 20 percent (Leviticus 6). A person was to first restore what was taken, and second, add one-fifth to it. Zacchaeus promised to repay those he had defrauded fourfold.

Consider the reaction from Jesus. He didn't just say, "Well, that's a nice gesture." No, Jesus said,

> Today salvation has come to this house, because he, too, is
> a son of Abraham. For the Son of Man has come to seek
> and to save that which was lost (Luke 19:9-10).

The point of these two stories from the Gospels isn't that Christians are to liquidate their wealth. But Jesus could see the true faith of a person by how they treated their possessions. As we will see throughout this book, what's important isn't so much the amount you own—rather, it's what owns you.

A biblical view of poverty

The Bible also has quite a bit to say about poverty. It puts the causes of poverty into four different categories. The first cause of poverty is *oppression and fraud.* In the Old Testament (for example, Proverbs 14:31; 22:7; 28:15) we find that many people were poor because they were oppressed by other individuals or by governments. Many times, governments established unjust laws or debased the currency, measures that resulted in the exploitation of individuals.

The second cause of poverty is *misfortune, persecution, or judgment.* In the book of Job we learn that God allowed Satan to test Job by bringing misfortune upon him (1:12-19). Elsewhere in the Old Testament (for example, Psalm 109:16; Isaiah 47:9; Lamentations 5:3) we read of misfortune or of God's judgment on a disobedient people.

When Israel turned from God's laws, God allowed foreign nations to take them into captivity as a judgment for their disobedience.

The third cause of poverty is *laziness, neglect, or gluttony.* Proverbs teaches that some people are poor because of improper habits and apathy (10:4; 13:4; 19:15; 20:13; 23:21).

The final cause of poverty is *the culture of poverty.* Proverbs 10:15 says, "The ruin of the poor is their poverty." Poverty breeds poverty, and the cycle is not easily broken. People who grow up in an impoverished culture usually lack the nutrition and the education that would enable them to rise out of poverty in the future.

The government's role in dealing with poverty

While government should not have to shoulder the entire responsibility for caring for the poor, it must take seriously the statements in Leviticus and Proverbs about defending the poor and fighting oppression. Government must not shirk its God-given responsibility to defend the poor from injustice. If government won't do this, or if the oppression is coming from the government itself, then Christians must exercise their prophetic voice and speak out against governmental abuse and misuse of power.

Government must first establish laws and statutes that prohibit and punish injustice. These laws should have significant penalties and be rigorously enforced so the poor are not exploited and defrauded. Second, government must provide a legal system that allows for the redress of grievances, allowing plaintiffs to bring their cases to court for settlement.

A second sphere for governmental action is in the area of misfortune. Many people slip into poverty through no fault of their own. In these cases, government must help distribute funds. Unfortunately, the track record of government programs isn't very impressive. The percentage of people living below the poverty level has essentially remained constant for decades despite the billions spent on poverty and welfare programs.

We need a welfare system that emphasizes work and initiative and does not foster dependency and laziness. One of the things integral to the Old Testament system and missing in our modern system of welfare is a *means test*. If people have true needs, we should help them. But when they are lazy and have poor work habits, we should admonish them to improve. Our welfare system often perpetuates poverty by failing to distinguish between those who have legitimate needs and those who need to be admonished in their sin.

The role of the church in dealing with poverty

The church has the potential to offer some unique solutions to poverty. Yet ever since the Depression in the 1930s and even more since the rise of the Great Society programs in the 1960s, the church has tended to abdicate its responsibility toward the poor to the government.

In the Old Testament, there were two means to help the poor. The first was through the gleaning laws listed in Leviticus 19:9-10 and Deuteronomy 24:19-22. As farmers reaped their crops, they would leave the corners of their fields unharvested. Also, anything that fell to the ground was left for the poor.

The second method used to help the poor was the tithe. In Leviticus 27:30 we find that the tithe provided funds that were "the Lord's." These funds supported both the priests and the poor. The funds were distributed by the priests to those who were truly needy.

In the New Testament, the church also had a role in helping meet the needs of the poor. In 1 Corinthians 16, Paul talks about a collection that was sent from the churches to the Jerusalem believers. We also find many scriptural admonitions calling for Christians to distribute their resources to others compassionately (2 Corinthians 9:7; 1 Timothy 5:9-10; 6:18; James 1:27).

Poverty is as much a psychological and spiritual problem as it is an economic problem, and it's in this realm that the church can be most effective. Although salvation is not the sole answer, the church and Christian organizations can meet the psychological and spiritual needs of poverty-stricken people. Most secular social programs don't place much emphasis on these needs and thus miss a crucial element in the solution to poverty.

Dual responsibility

The verses concerning the gleaning laws and the tithe seem to indicate that both the government and the church should be involved in helping the poor. Ideally, the church should be in the vanguard of this endeavor. Unfortunately, the church has neglected its responsibility, and government is now heavily involved in poverty relief.

As we have noted, one of the causes of poverty is the culture of poverty. People are poor because they are poor. An individual who grows up in a culture of poverty is destined for a life of poverty unless something dramatic takes place. Poor nutrition, poor education, poor work habits, and poor family relationships can easily condemn an individual to perpetual poverty, poverty that the person will then perpetuate to the next generation.

Here's where the church can provide some answers. First, in the area of capital investment, churches should develop a mercy fund to help those in need. Christians should reach out to those in poverty by distributing their own financial resources and by supporting ministries working in this area. Such an outreach provides churches with a mechanism to meet the physical needs of the poor as well as a context to meet their spiritual needs.

A second solution is for Christians to use their gifts and abilities to help those caught in the web of poverty. Doctors can provide health care. Educators can provide literacy and remedial reading programs. Businesspeople can impart job skills.

Third, this kind of social involvement can also provide opportunities for evangelism. Social action and evangelism often work hand in hand. When we meet people's needs, we often open up opportunities to reach them for Jesus Christ.

Christian involvement can often lead to spiritual conversion. By bringing people into a relationship with Jesus Christ, we can break the culture of poverty. Second Corinthians 5:17 says that we become new creatures in Jesus Christ. Being born again can improve attitudes and family relationships. It can give people new direction and the ability to overcome handicaps and hardships.

A fourth area of Christian involvement is to call people to their biblical task. Proverbs 6:6 says, "Go to the ant, O sluggard, observe her ways and be wise." We are to admonish laziness and poor habits that lead to poverty. In the New Testament, Paul reminds the Thessalonians of their church rule: "If anyone is not willing to work, then he is not to eat, either" (2 Thessalonians 3:10). Christians should gently but firmly admonish those whose poverty is the result of poor work habits to begin taking responsibility for their own lives.

The church can help those addicted to alcohol or other drugs to overcome their dependencies. Christians can work to heal broken families. Dealing with these root causes will help solve the poverty problem.

What should the Christian's lifestyle be?

What, then, does this biblical view of wealth and poverty have to say about the way Christians should live? A brief survey of Scripture shows godly people living in a variety of different economic situations. For example, Daniel served as secretary of state in pagan administrations and no doubt had what could be called an affluent lifestyle. Ezekiel lived outside the city in what might have been considered a middle-class lifestyle. And Jeremiah essentially lived a lower-class lifestyle.

Which prophet best honored God with his lifestyle? The question is of course ridiculous. Each man honored God and followed God's leading in his life. Yet each lived a very different lifestyle.

Christians must reject the assumption implicit in many discussions about economic lifestyle. There is no ideal one for Christians.

One size doesn't fit all. Instead, we must seek the Lord to discern His will and calling in our lives.

As we do this, there are some biblical principles that will guide us. First, we should acknowledge that God is the Creator of all that we own and use. Whether we're rich or poor, we must acknowledge His provision in our lives. We are stewards of the creation; the Earth is ultimately the Lord's (see Psalm 24:1).

Second, we should "seek first His kingdom and His righteousness" (Matthew 6:33). We must recognize and avoid the dangers of wealth. Greed isn't an exclusive attribute of the rich, nor is covetousness an exclusive attribute of the poor. Christians must guard against the effect of wealth on their spiritual lives. There is nothing wrong with owning possessions. The problem comes when, as previously noted, the possessions own *us*.

Third, Christians must recognize the freedom that comes with simplicity. A simple lifestyle can free us from the dangers of being owned by material possessions. It can also free us for a deeper spiritual life. While simplicity isn't an end in itself, it can be a means to a spiritual life of service.

Here are a few suggestions on how to begin living a simple lifestyle. First, *eat sensibly and eat less*. This includes observing not only good nutrition, but occasional times for prayer and fasting. Use the time saved for prayer and meditation on God's Word. Use the money saved for world hunger relief.

Second, *dress modestly*. This not only obeys the biblical injunction about modesty, but avoids the temptation of consumerism, which requires us to purchase new wardrobes as styles change. A moderate and modest wardrobe can endure the drastic swings of fashion.

Third, *give all you can*. The famous Methodist preacher John Wesley had a simple recipe for a proper biblical perspective on money: Earn all you can, save all you can, and give all you can:

- Concerning earning, Wesley said, "Gain all you can by honest industry. Use all possible diligence in your calling.

Lose no time. If you understand yourself and your relation to God and man, you know you have none to spare."

- On saving money, he said, "Do not waste any part of so precious a talent merely in gratifying the desire of the eye by superfluous or expensive apparel, or by needless ornaments."

- He also admonished us to be generous in our giving. If we merely hoard our money, "You may as well throw your money into the sea, as bury it in the earth. And you may as well bury it in the earth, as in your chest, or in the Bank of England."[1]

Look for opportunities to give the resources God has blessed you with. If God has blessed you with wealth, look for opportunities to give it away prudently. If God has blessed you with great abilities, use them for His glory.

In the next few chapters we'll talk about giving, saving, and spending. But before that we need to address the issue of materialism and consumerism.

2

Materialism *and* Consumerism

Do we live in a materialistic culture? Most people would agree that we do. By materialism, we mean the excessive interest in and desire for money or possessions. Certainly that would describe our culture.

Most Americans don't have a biblical view about materialism and material goods. For example, a survey by George Barna found that 72 percent believe that people are blessed by God so they can enjoy life as much as possible. And 81 percent believe the Bible teaches that God helps those who help themselves.[1]

By contrast the Old Testament teaches that we're blessed by God in order to be a blessing to others (Genesis 12:1-2), and that we should rely upon God rather than ourselves (Psalm 37:39-40). Jesus taught in Matthew 6:24-25,

> No one can serve two masters. Either he will hate the one and love the other, or he will be devoted to the one and despise the other. You cannot serve both God and money.
> For this reason I say to you, do not be worried about your life, what you will eat or what you will drink; nor for your body, as to what you will put on. Is not life more than food, and the body more than clothing?

Jesus is warning us that we can be in bondage to material possessions, and He tells us we can't serve both material goods and God.

The Bible also warns us that accumulating wealth can bring specific temptations. The fifth chapter of James and the book of Amos describe how financial power can lead to economic injustice as well as various forms of oppression.

Dangers of materialism

The Bible warns about the dangers of materialism. First, *materialism feeds our greed*. We're never satisfied with what we have—instead, we want more. Jesus tells the parable of a rich man who decides to tear down his barns and build bigger ones (Luke 12:18). He's not satisfied with his current situation but is striving to make it better. Today most of us have adjusted to a life of affluence as normal. In fact, many are striving to have even more than they have right now. This is one of the dangers of materialism.

Second, *materialism creates divided loyalties*. We just saw this in the passage from Matthew 6. We can also see this in Paul's letter to Timothy about not being divided in the Christian life. "No soldier in active service entangles himself in the affairs of everyday life, so that he may please the one who enlisted him as a soldier" (2 Timothy 2:4). John warns us,

> Do not love the world nor the things in the world. If anyone loves the world, the love of the Father is not in him (1 John 2:15).

Third, *materialism can dull God's direction in our lives*. Once we have adjusted to a lifestyle of comfort, it is difficult to surrender our will to God (to go on the mission field, to go into Christian ministry, and so on). Part of the problem is that materialism breeds discontent. We want more of the world and its possessions rather than more of God and His will in our lives. What a contrast to what Paul says in Philippians, where he counts all things to be loss (3:7-8) and instead has learned to be content (4:11). He goes on to talk about "godliness with contentment" in 1 Timothy 6:6-7. Contentment is an effective antidote to materialism.

Fourth, *materialism can also lead to pride and arrogance.* Proverbs 28:11 says, "The rich man is wise in his own eyes." A wealthy man believes he has achieved his success by himself and therefore has a proud heart. Ezekiel 28:4-5 says,

> By your wisdom and understanding you have gained wealth for yourself and amassed gold and silver in your treasuries. By your great skill in trading you have increased your wealth, and because of your wealth your heart has grown proud (NIV).

Jeremiah 9:3 says that materialistic people act as if they don't even know God. In fact, the Proverbs talk about how wealth tempts us to forget about Him.

> Keep deception and lies far from me, give me neither poverty nor riches; feed me with the food that is my portion, that I not be full and deny You and say, "Who is the Lord?" Or that I not be in want and steal, and profane the name of my God (Proverbs 30:8-9).

Hosea 13:6 also talks about how wealth tempts us to forget about God: "As they had their pasture, they became satisfied, and being satisfied, their heart became proud; therefore they forgot Me."

Materialism does not satisfy. Solomon had access to wealth (gold, silver, possessions) and pleasure (slaves, harems) like few other men. He says he denied nothing to himself and refused his heart no pleasure (Ecclesiastes 2:10). He concludes that the more money or wealth you have, the more you want, because there's never enough (Ecclesiastes 5:10).

But there's a more basic issue driving the materialism in our society, and that is *consumerism.* Consumerism is much more than mere materialism. It is a way of perceiving the world that has affected all of us—young and old, rich and poor, believer and nonbeliever in significant ways. How has it affected us, and how has it affected the church? These are questions we will address in this chapter.

Is America suffering from "affluenza"?

The authors of the book *Affluenza* have been concerned that their meaning has sometimes been misapplied. They point out that writers often use their term *affluenza* with different emphases. Some use it to talk about the spoiled children of the super-rich. Others apply it to what they call "sudden-wealth syndrome."

However, the authors intend it to be applied to a much broader perspective. They say that the virus of affluenza "is not confined to the upper classes but has found its way throughout our society. Its symptoms affect the poor as well as the rich...Affluenza infects all of us, though in different ways."[2]

They go on to say that "the Affluenza epidemic is rooted in the obsessive, almost religious quest for economic expansion that has become the core principle of what is called the American dream."[3]

Affluenza is rooted in a number of key concepts. First, it's rooted in the belief that the measure of national progress lies in the gross domestic product. Second, it's rooted in the idea that each generation must do better economically than the previous one. Thus, when economic realities should be restraining our spending (both as a nation and as individuals), we pursue a plan of "buy now and pay later" in order to expand economically.

> **More wealth brings more worry**
>
> When your goods increase, Solomon says, the number of those who wish to consume them increases as well (Ecclesiastes 5:11). He even goes on to add that the wealth and the abundance of a rich man doesn't allow him to sleep (Ecclesiastes 5:12). In other words, the more you have, the more you have to worry about.

Anyone looking at some of the social statistics for the U.S. might conclude that our priorities are out of whack. We spend more on shoes, jewelry, and watches than on higher education. We spend much more on auto maintenance than on religious and welfare activities. And three times as many Americans buy Christmas presents for their pets as buy presents for their neighbors.[4]

Debt and waste also show skewed priorities. More Americans have declared personal bankruptcy than have graduated from college. Our annual production of solid waste would fill a convoy of garbage trucks stretching halfway to the moon. We have twice as many shopping centers as high schools.[5]

And Americans seem to be working themselves to death in order to pay for everything they own or want to buy. We now work more hours each year than do the citizens of any other industrialized country, including Japan. And according to Department of Labor statistics, full-time American workers are putting in 160 hours more (essentially one month more) per year than they did in 1969.[6] And 95 percent of our workers say they wish they could spend more time with their families.[7]

Americans do recognize the problem and are trying to simplify their lives. A 2004 poll by the Center for a New American Dream showed a change in attitudes and action. The poll revealed that 85 percent of Americans think our priorities are out of whack. For example, nearly nine in ten (88 percent) said American society is too materialistic. They also found that most Americans (93 percent) feel we are too focused on working and making money. They also believed (91 percent) that we buy and consume more than we need. More than half of Americans (52 percent) said they have too much debt.[8]

The poll found that many Americans were taking steps to work less, even if that meant reducing their consuming. Nearly half of Americans (48 percent) said they had voluntarily made changes in their lives in order to get more time and have a less stressful life. This increase in the number of self-proclaimed "down-shifters" suggests the beginning of a national change in priorities.

Perhaps Americans are coming to the realization that more consumer goods don't make them happy. Think back to the year 1957. That was the year that the program *Leave It to Beaver* premiered on television. It was also the year that the Russians shot *Sputnik* into space. That was a long time ago.

But 1957 is significant for another reason. It was in that year that the percentage of Americans who described themselves as "very happy" reached a plateau.[9] Since then there has been an ever-declining percentage of Americans who describe themselves that way...even though the size of the average home today is twice what it was in the 1950s, and these homes are filled with consumer electronics someone back then could only dream about.

How can we find margin in a culture suffering from "affluenza"?

One person who has provided a biblical prescription for dealing with materialism, consumerism, and affluenza is Dr. Richard Swenson. He sets forth his answers in his book *Margin: How to Create the Emotional, Physical, Financial, and Time Reserves You Need.*[10] He believes that affluenza is a major disease and talks about how we got to this point. He also talks about how we find ourselves today on overload and how we should deal with it in *The Overload Syndrome: Learning to Live Within Your Limits.*[11]

Swenson defines margin as "the space that once existed between ourselves and our limits." We should have margin between our load and our limits. If your load is lower than your limits, then you have margin. If your load exceeds your limits, you are on overload. He argues that progress in our modern world incessantly chews up margin. Essentially the pace of modern life has been stoked by progress. He also argues that the speed of change is accelerating.

All of this causes stress, which many have chosen to call "the stress of excess." The pace of life is accelerating, and the number of choices is increasing. In my book *Signs of Warning, Signs of Hope*, I talked about the coming crisis of priorities that would be due to too many choices and too little time.[12] Today we live in a world of "overchoice." Alvin Toffler said in his book *Future Shock* that overchoice occurs when "the advantages of diversity and individualization are canceled by the complexity of buyers' decision-making process."[13]

We can see all sorts of signs of overchoice. Walk down the cereal aisle in a grocery story. Look at the wall of televisions—regular and flat screens—in an electronics store. We have more and more choices.

Not only do we have too many choices, we also have less time. Sure, we all have 24 hours. But we have less leisure time or discretionary time. Most of us live a fast-paced, frenetic lifestyle. We are making more and more choices in less and less time.

This "time famine" creates stress. Richard Swenson points out that if you look at all the countries that have the most prosperity, they're also the ones with the most stress. He uses a great illustration of how we react to additions to our schedule (boss asks if you can work overtime, church asks if you can teach Sunday school, spouse suggests you go out

> ### Overchoice
>
> Sometimes the choices we have become ridiculous. There are more than 19,000 ways you can order Starbucks coffee, and you even have five kinds of milk to stir into it (whole, nonfat, half-and-half, organic, and soy).[14] And if you consider all the various colors, styles, and options for cars, you have 25 million versions you can choose.[15]

to dinner with the neighbors). Our reaction when our lives are 80 percent full (on the unsaturated side of our limits) is usually positive. But our reaction is very different when our lives are 100 percent full or 120 percent full (oversaturated). The questions in each example are the same, but the reactions are very different.[16]

And we certainly live in a world of overload. Swenson talks about different types of overload: activity overload, choice overload, information overload, technology overload, and work overload. The one that's most significant here is *possession overload*, which is the problem of having too much. Swenson says,

> Possession overload is the kind of problem where you have so many things you find your life is being taken up with maintaining and caring for things instead of people.

Acquiring more things doesn't fill your life with happiness; it just fills your life. "Tragedy," observes Swenson, "is wanting something badly, getting it, and finding it empty."[17]

In his books, Swenson gives lots of practical suggestions on how to build margin into our lives and how to live a life with less stress and more simplicity. His first book talks about how to develop margin in emotional energy, physical energy, time, and finances.

A key element in dealing with materialism and consumerism is contentment. Paul writes that godliness with contentment is great gain (1 Timothy 6:6). We should be willing to pursue godly contentment rather than riches. In another epistle, Paul says that he has "learned the secret of being content in any and every situation, whether well fed or hungry, whether living in plenty or in want" (Philippians 4:12 NIV). That should be our goal as well.

How should we respond to materialism and consumerism?

As we have already seen, we live in a culture that encourages us to buy more and more. No longer are we encouraged to live within our means. We are tempted to buy more than just the necessities and spend more on luxuries. The Bible warns us about this. Proverbs 21:17 says, "He who loves pleasure will become a poor man; he who loves wine and oil will not become rich."

In our lifetimes we have lots of money flow through our hands, and we need to make wiser choices. Consider that a person who makes just $25,000 a year will in his lifetime have a million dollars pass through his hands. The median family income in America is twice that. That means that two million dollars will pass through the average American family's hands.

A tragic aspect of consumerism is that there's never enough. There's always the desire for more because each purchase satisfies for only a short while. Then there's the need for more and more. Essentially, it's the law of diminishing returns. Economists use a more technical term (the law of diminishing marginal return). Simply put, the more we get, the less it satisfies and the more we want.

Once again the Bible warns us about this. Haggai 1:5-6 says,

> Thus says the LORD of hosts, "Consider your ways! You have sown much, but harvest little; you eat, but there is not enough to be satisfied; you drink, but there is not enough to become drunk; you put on clothing, but no one is warm enough; and he who earns, earns wages to put into a purse with holes."

We should also be responsible citizens. But a tragic consequence of consumerism is what it does to the average citizen. James Kuntsler, author of *The Geography of Nowhere*, believes we have "mutated from citizens to consumers." He says that "consumers have no duties or responsibilities or obligations to their fellow consumers. Citizens do. They have the obligation to care about their fellow citizens and about the integrity of the town's environment and history."[18]

Lonely consumers

America was once a nation of joiners. In the 1830s Alexis de Tocqueville noted this in his book *Democracy in America*. Americans would join in all sorts of voluntary associations. But we seem to no longer be joiners but loners. Sure, there are still many people volunteering and giving their time. But much of this is "on the run" as we shuttle from place to place in our busy lives.

Christians are called to be the salt of the earth (Matthew 5:13) and the light of the world (Matthew 5:14-16). We are also called to be ambassadors for Christ (2 Corinthians 5:20). We must resist the temptations of consumerism that encourage us to focus on ourselves and withdraw from active involvement in society.

What about the health-and-wealth gospel?

Before we conclude this chapter, it's worth discussing a Christianized version of materialism and consumerism. It has been referred to as the "health-and-wealth gospel" or the "prosperity gospel." The premise is simple. God wants Christians to be healthy and wealthy. It's God's will for us to prosper, and we should therefore claim God's promises for these things. That's why some have even called this the "name-it-and-claim-it gospel."

This is a significant movement in America. A poll that appeared in the September 2006 issue of *Time* magazine documented American attitudes on the prosperity gospel. Approximately 17 percent of Christians surveyed said they considered themselves part of such a movement. And nearly two-thirds (61 percent) believed that God wants people to be prosperous.[19]

The primary scriptural justification for this belief is Galatians 3:13, which says, "Christ redeemed us from the curse of the Law, having become a curse for us—for it is written, 'Cursed is everyone who hangs on a tree.'" According to the prosperity-gospel view, when Jesus died, He died to redeem us from the curse of the law—and one of those curses was poverty, which results from the curse of the fall of Adam (Genesis 3).

Proponents of this view therefore argue that the gospel of Jesus Christ set us free from sickness and poverty. We now have restored fellowship with God through Jesus Christ and thus have access to God's abundant provisions.

Another passage often used by those who teach a prosperity gospel is 3 John 2. In this letter, the apostle John expresses his desire that Gaius "may prosper and be in good health, just as your soul prospers." Proponents argue that if it's God's will for us to prosper, then we should claim God's promise by faith. Those who teach a prosperity gospel also sometimes quote even John 10:10, in which Jesus says, "I came that they may have life, and have it abundantly."

A proper biblical interpretation of each of these verses is important. In Galatians 3:13, the clear teaching is that eternal life is available for all through faith in Jesus Christ. And there will be blessings that accompany our faith. But as we will see in the chapter on giving (chapter 3), some of these blessings may be material, but most of them will be spiritual. Paul isn't promising us health and wealth in this passage. We can see that clearly in the next verse (3:14), which says, "...so that we would receive the promise of the Spirit through faith." The context is faith. Paul is reminding the Galatians of the spiritual blessing of salvation, not the material blessing of wealth and prosperity. Yes, Jesus died and redeemed us from the curse of the law. But that doesn't mean that faithful believers will always experience health, wealth, and worldly success.

The passage in 3 John 2 is not a promise or a guarantee. It merely reflects John's desire for Gaius to do well. In fact, the Greek word for "prosper" could just as easily be translated "to go well." Again, the context is key. It is not John's intent to teach doctrine in this verse. He is merely wishing that things go well with his friend. This greeting and well-wishing from John is not a universal promise to be claimed by Christians.

The passage in John 10:10 has nothing to do with wealth or prosperity. When Jesus promises an abundant life, He's talking about the Christian life and the gospel. He isn't promising that once you become a Christian you will become wealthy.

It's also worth noting that some proponents of the prosperity gospel misinterpret 2 Corinthians 8:9, which says, "You know the grace of our Lord Jesus Christ, that though He was rich, yet for your sake He became poor, so that you through His poverty might become rich." Yet again, the context of the passage is key. Paul was not saying that Christ died so we might become wealthy and prosperous. If anything, he was teaching just the opposite. In the context, he is encouraging the Christians in Corinth to give generously because of what Christ accomplished in His death, burial, and resurrection.

Further, when we look at the lives of Jesus' disciples in the New Testament, we don't see them experiencing a prosperity gospel. If anything, they're experiencing an "adversity gospel." All were persecuted, and most of them died martyrs' deaths. Consider the adversity that Paul faced, which he described in 2 Corinthians 11:24-27:

> Five times I received from the Jews the forty lashes minus one. Three times I was beaten with rods, once I was stoned, three times I was shipwrecked, I spent a night and a day in the open sea, I have been constantly on the move. I have been in danger from rivers, in danger from bandits, in danger from my own countrymen, in danger from Gentiles; in danger in the city, in danger in the country, in danger at sea; and in danger from false brothers. I have labored and toiled and have often gone without sleep; I have known hunger and thirst and have often gone without food; I have been cold and naked (NIV).

The prosperity gospel is based upon incorrect interpretations of these biblical passages. It is guilty of imposing a faulty understanding of grace, giving, and faith upon these passages in order to justify a gospel of health and wealth. And we certainly don't see evidence of a prosperity gospel in the lives of the disciples.

～

Now that we've discussed materialism and consumerism, let's turn our attention to the biblical and practical aspect of making the most of our money in tough times. In the next few chapters we'll talk about giving, debt, saving, and spending. As we've already seen in this chapter, we need to establish the proper biblical priorities in these areas.

3

Giving

In order to further develop a biblical point of view on money, we should put priority on the subject of giving. A proper view of giving provides the framework for a proper view of saving, investing, and debt.

Giving is an important topic because there's so much misinformation and misunderstanding about it. Should Christians give a tithe? What's the relationship between the Old Testament tithe and New Testament giving? Where should our giving go? And how can we determine whether an organization is worthy of our gifts? These are important questions we'll try to answer in this chapter.

How are the tithe and charitable giving related?

In order to understand the relationship between the Old Testament tithe and New Testament giving, we need to begin with the teaching about the tithe. The Old Testament principle of the tithe provides the foundation for New Testament giving.

The word tithe means "a tenth part." Once you understand this, you realize that many people use the word *tithe*, but aren't really accurate in using it. Someone who, say, makes $3000 a month and gives only $100 a month is not tithing. One study found that only 3 percent of households tithe their income to their church.[1]

The principle of the tithe can be found in Leviticus 27:30, which says, "A tithe of everything from the land, whether grain from the soil or fruit from the trees, belongs to the LORD; it is holy to the LORD" (NIV). We can derive three principles from this passage: 1) The tithe was applied to "everything from the land" and didn't apply to just some income or wealth. 2) The tithe "belongs to the LORD" and not to the people. And 3) The tithe is holy—that is, it's set apart and should be given to the Lord.

What if a believer in the Old Testament did not tithe? The answer to that question can be found in Malachi 3:8-10:

> "Will a man rob God? Yet you are robbing Me! But you say, 'How have we robbed You?' In tithes and offerings. You are cursed with a curse, for you are robbing Me, the whole nation of you! Bring the whole tithe into the store-house, so that there may be food in My house, and test Me now in this," says the LORD of hosts, "if I will not open for you the windows of heaven and pour out for you a blessing until it overflows."

If the nation of Israel refused to pay the tithe, then they were considered guilty of robbing God. The Israelites were to bring the whole tithe into the storehouse, not just part of the tithe.

In the Old Testament, the tithe was not voluntary but mandatory. Two kinds of giving are taught in the Bible: giving to the government (compulsory) and giving to God (voluntary). Israel was not only a spiritual community but a nation. The tithe was necessary to fund the nation. That is why many have referred to the tithe as a precursor to taxes. Israel was a theocracy, and the priests were the leaders of the government. They were supported by the tithe.

Firstfruits

The firstfruits applied to the vineyard (Leviticus 19:23-25) as well as to the production of grain and the fruit from fruit trees (Exodus 23:16). It also applied to any coarse meal (Numbers 15:20-21) and other produce (2 Chronicles 31:5).

There were actually three tithes.

- One tithe was for the priests and Levites: "A tithe of everything from the land, whether grain from the soil or fruit from the trees, belongs to the LORD" (Leviticus 27:30). This was paid to the Levites, who in turn gave a tenth of that to the priests (Numbers 18:26). This would be similar to the New Testament giving that goes toward ministry.

- The second tithe provided funds for the Jewish festival (Deuteronomy 12:17-18).

- A third tithe was to provide support for the widows, orphans, and poor (Deuteronomy 14:28).

The first two tithes were regularly collected, while the last one was collected every third year. Thus, the total amount of tithe was approximately 23 percent each year.

The tithe in the Old Testament was to be given from the first-fruits. Proverbs 3:9 says: "Honor the LORD from your wealth, and from the first of all you produce." The tithe was to be the first and the best of the crop, not an afterthought.

Freewill offerings in the Old Testament

Although the Old Testament tithe was mandatory, all other giving was voluntary (Exodus 25; 1 Chronicles 29). Each person gave according to what they felt led to give. There was no percentage. Some of these gifts were referred to as "freewill offerings" (Leviticus 22; Numbers 15; Deuteronomy 12).

One example of this was when Moses challenged the people of Israel to give to the construction of the tabernacle. They were so enthusiastic that they had to be "restrained from bringing any more. For the material they had was sufficient and more than enough" (Exodus 36:6-7).

Another example of this was the freewill offerings collected when the temple was rebuilt. We read in the Old Testament book of Ezra that the people were encouraged to give a "freewill offering" for "the house of the LORD which is in Jerusalem." These were voluntary gifts of gold and silver and cattle and other valuables (Ezra 1:6).

As we can see, the concept of voluntary giving didn't begin in the New Testament. There are a few examples of it in the Old Testament.

Where should the tithe go?

In the Old Testament, the answer to the question of where the tithes should go was very clear. The tithe was to go to the storehouse. In other words, it went to the temple and was used to support the priests and Levites.

Today we don't have a temple, but many pastors teach that the local church is the storehouse. Although this seems like a good historical parallel, there is nothing in the New Testament that designates the church as the storehouse. The closest we have is in Acts 2, where the believers gave money to the apostles, who used godly wisdom to distribute it.

It seems logical, however, that our firstfruits should go to the local church. That doesn't preclude supporting worthwhile parachurch ministries as well. Although the church is not the storehouse, it often serves as a clearinghouse in the distribution of funds to missionaries and various parachurch organizations.

The value of the tithe is that it reminds us that God owns it all. It's not merely an afterthought or a tip. We are to give Him the firstfruits of our labor as a reminder that all we have is ultimately from Him.

God even challenged the Israelites to test Him and go back to tithing. It was a divine invitation for them (and us) to rest on God's promises that He will provide for our needs (Malachi 3:8-12).

Is the tithe taught in the New Testament?

Nowhere in the New Testament is there an explicit command to tithe. The primary reason is that the tithe was for the Levites and the priests. The substitutionary death of Christ for our sins did away with the need for a temple. Christians don't need the temple and don't need priests as intercessors. We are all priests now and no longer live under law but under grace (Romans 6:15).

New Testament believers are never commanded to tithe. They are instructed to pay their taxes (Romans 13:1-7). That is the only *required* giving in the church age.

Christians are to give to those who suffer (1 Corinthians 16:1; Galatians 2:10). We are to give to those who trust God to supply their needs (Philippians 4:19). We are to give as God has prospered us (1 Corinthians 16:2) and are to give cheerfully (2 Corinthians 9:7). And the Bible teaches that we will ultimately give account of our stewardship (Romans 14:12).

The first-century believers set a high standard for giving. They sold their goods and gave money to any believer in need (Acts 2:45). They sold their property and gave the entire amount to the work of the apostles (Acts 4:36–5:2). And they also gave generously to the ministry of Paul (2 Corinthians 8:1-5) on a continual basis (Philippians 4:16-18).

Even though the tithe was no longer required, it appears that the early believers used the tithe as a baseline for their giving. After all, a large majority of the first-century believers were Jewish, and so they gave not only the tithe but above and beyond the 10 percent. Some of the early church fathers even felt the tithe *should* be required because it was an essential duty for all Christians.

Paul makes it clear that Christians are not to give "grudgingly or under compulsion" but as each believer has "purposed in his heart" (2 Corinthians 9:7). So the tithe was no longer the mandatory requirement, but it appeared to provide a basis for voluntary giving by believers.

Should you tithe on your gross income or net income?

A quick answer I often give to the question "Should you tithe the gross or net income?" is to ask whether someone wants God to bless their gross income or their net income. That little quip often clears up the matter quickly. Since we are no longer under law but grace, we should rightly consider what we do in terms of giving to ministry and the blessing we will receive. Now, we shouldn't give to get. But if you are looking for a blessing in giving, then ask yourself what you want God to bless. The point is that most Christians seem to be more interested in cutting corners with their finances rather than in following what God set out as a model for giving in the Bible.

Many early Church Fathers taught that Christians should tithe

Irenaeus: "The Jews were constrained to a regular payment of tithes; Christians, who have liberty, assign all their possessions to the Lord, bestowing freely not the portions of their property, since they have the hope of greater things."

Jerome: "If anyone shall not do this [pay their tithe] he is convicted of defrauding and supplanting God."

Augustine: "Tithes are required as a matter of debt, and he who has been unwilling to give them has been guilty of robbery." [2]

If the Old Testament example of the tithe applied to everything, then the answer to the "gross or net" question should be obvious. What financial benefits do you receive? This would not only include your gross income but other benefits (insurance, retirement benefits, stock options, and so on).

Many Christians take the meaning of tithe literally and give one-tenth of their income back to the Lord. Others see it as a baseline and give more than that as a sacrificial, freewill offering. The place to start is to look at your gross income and give back to the Lord as you purpose in your heart (2 Corinthians 9:7).

How do age and income affect giving?

A number of years ago, Barna Research did a study of giving by Christians. They found that less than 10 percent of born-again Christians gave 10 percent to their church. They also found that age and annual income were significant indicators of giving.

For example, they found that the younger you are, the less likely you were to give. The "builder" generation (born before 1946) were the most likely to give to a church within a given month. The boomers (born 1946 to 1964) were less likely to give. And "busters" (born after 1964) were the least likely to give.[3]

Income was also significant. Barna Research found that the more money a person makes, the less likely he or she is to tithe:

> While 8 percent of those making $20,000 or less gave at least 10 percent of their income to churches, that proportion dropped to 5 percent among those in the $20,000-$29,999 and $30,000-$39,999 categories; to 4 percent among those in the $40,000-$59,999 range, down to 2 percent for those in the $60,000-$74,999 niche; and to 1 percent for those making $75,000-$99,999.[4]

How should Christians give?

Christians are commanded to give, and so the real question we need to answer is *how* they should give. As we've seen, not all Christians give the same amount, and sadly many Christians do not give anything to their church or to Christian organizations. So let's look at a few key principles that should guide our giving.

The first principle is, *when you sow generously, you will reap generously,* as 2 Corinthians 9:6 says: "He who sows sparingly will also reap sparingly, and he who sows bountifully will also reap bountifully." Elsewhere in Scripture, we read that the size of a harvest corresponds to what we scatter. Proverbs 11:24-25 says,

> There is one who scatters, and yet increases all the more,
> And there is one who withholds what is justly due, and yet
> it results only in want. The generous man will be prosper-
> ous, and he who waters will himself be watered.

Of course a spiritual harvest may differ from the kind of seed that's sown. For example, a material seed (giving to ministry) may reap a spiritual harvest (1 Corinthians 9:9-10).

God has blessed us both materially (Acts 14:17) and spiritually (Roman 5:17). So we can be assured that He will increase our harvest. "He who supplies seed to the sower and bread for food will supply and multiply your seed for sowing and increase the harvest of your righteousness" (2 Corinthians 9:10).

As we've seen, a second principle is, *we are to give according to what we have purposed in our hearts,* as 2 Corinthians 9:7 says: "Each one must do just as he has purposed in his heart, not grudgingly or under compulsion, for God loves a cheerful giver." Your giving should be a deliberate act and not just a quick response to some emotional appeal. Certainly there's nothing wrong with giving a freewill offering because God has moved you to support a particular missionary or project. But we should also have a purpose and a plan to our giving.

A third principle is, *we are to give voluntarily.* We are told, again in 2 Corinthians 9:7, that we aren't to give under guilt or compulsion.

Direct payment

Many Christians have begun to give through an automatic deduction from their checking account. This has the positive effect of providing regular support for the church or Christian organizations. The monthly amount is deducted whether you are actively thinking about the ministry or not. The possible negative effect is that it could become so automatic that you forget about the ministry and fail to pray for it.

That admonition does not mean that we are to support the local church or Christian organizations only when we feel like it. In this particular passage, Paul was challenging believers in Corinth to give to a special need (the financial needs of the believers in Jerusalem). This was a one-time special offering that was above and beyond providing for the regular needs of the church in Corinth.

Fourth, *we are also to give generously.* As mentioned, in 2 Corinthians 9:7 it says, "God loves a cheerful giver." He values not the size of the gift (Acts 11:29; 1 Corinthians 16:2) but the heart of the giver (not reluctantly or grudgingly) and the willingness of the giver (a cheerful giver).

We see that principle played out in the Old Testament. When the temple needed to be rebuilt, Joash put an offering box out for those who would give to this important work. Second Chronicles 24:10 says, "All the officials and all the people brought their contributions gladly, dropping them into the chest until it was full" (NIV). Notice that it says they gave *gladly* to the rebuilding of the temple. They provided a model for what Paul calls a "cheerful giver."

Fifth, *we are also to give sacrificially.* As Paul was writing to the church in Corinth, he told them of the sacrificial giving of the Macedonian Christians. He said,

> In a great ordeal of affliction their abundance of joy and their deep poverty overflowed in the wealth of their liberality. For I testify that according to their ability, and beyond their ability, they gave of their own accord (2 Corinthians 8:2-3).

Consider that on the one hand Paul is talking about their "deep poverty" but then goes on to say that they still gave "beyond their ability." I don't know too many people who today are giving beyond their ability. I know quite a few people who are giving less than their ability. And I have had many people call into my radio program telling me that they can't afford to tithe. In this passage, Paul challenges the believers in Corinth (and by extension challenges us) to re-evaluate our priorities and give sacrificially.

Once again we can see this principle at work in the Old Testament as well. David balked at giving a sacrifice to the Lord that wasn't really his sacrifice to give. In 2 Samuel 24:24 David says, "I will not offer burnt offerings to the LORD my God which cost me nothing." David is reminding us by his behavior that true sacrificial giving means being willing to sacrifice that which we would be inclined to keep for ourselves.

∼

When handling money, we should make sure that we have the right priorities. Giving back to the Lord is an important first priority. Christian giving is a part of biblical stewardship. We are to be faithful and trustworthy stewards (1 Corinthians 4:2).

We begin with the acknowledgment that God owns everything (1 Corinthians 10:25) and that we are merely giving back to Him a portion of what we hold in our hands. Essentially, we are merely His money managers. He holds us accountable for everything He provides (Romans 14:12).

We should also make sure our earthly and heavenly priorities are in proper order. Jesus admonished us to store up treasures in heaven (Matthew 6:20). As we now discuss debt, credit, saving, investing, and spending, it's important that we keep our biblical priorities straight.

4

Debt *and* Credit

Not only is it important for us to have a proper perspective on giving, it's also important to have a proper perspective concerning debt. Before we can apply biblical principles concerning economics and finances, we need to put the problem of debt in perspective.

You can't overemphasize the impact of debt on our society. It's a leading cause for divorce and also the reason for trouble in many more marriages. It's also one of the causes of depression as well as suicide. People in debt don't start out to ruin their lives and the lives of their families, but the consequences are often devastating.

The high level of personal indebtedness in this country is a relatively recent phenomenon. Less than a century ago, credit cards were unknown, and car loans were a rarity. Home mortgages were unusual too, and they really began to proliferate only when GIs returning from the War wanted to buy their own homes.

If you were to bring a person from the middle of the twentieth century to our time and tell them about all the debts the typical American has, they would shake their head. They wouldn't even believe the number of people with credit-card debt or the number of people who finance a car loan. And they would be even more amazed that banks and the government lend tens of thousands of dollars to college students before they're even able to prove they can earn enough to pay back the loans on time.

The Bible and debt

The Bible has quite a bit to say about money, and a significant part of it is warnings about debt. Proverbs 22:7 says, "The rich rule over the poor, and the borrower is a servant to the lender" (NIV). When you borrow money and put yourself in debt, you put yourself in a situation where the lender has significant influence over you.

> ### "No" to credit
>
> J.C. Penney opened his first store in 1902. He lived up to his name (James *Cash* Penney) and accepted "cash only" for his goods. He disliked credit, and it wasn't until 1959 that the J.C. Penney stores started issuing credit cards.

Many other verses in the Proverbs also warn about the danger of taking on debt, especially another person's debt (Proverbs 17:18; 22:26-27; 27:13). While this does not mean that we can never be in debt, it does warn us about its dangers.

God actually intended for the nation of Israel to be a lender, not a borrower. Deuteronomy 28:12 says,

> The LORD will open for you His good storehouse, the heavens, to give rain to your land in its season and bless all the work of your hand; and you shall lend to many nations, but you shall not borrow.

If you are debt-free you're free to follow the Lord's leading in your life. If you're in debt, you're constrained and become a servant to the lender. People who are in financial bondage are not emotionally or spiritually free. Their financial obligations weigh heavy upon their mind and spirit.

What about taking on another's debt obligations? This is called *surety*—when a person agrees to be responsible for the debt or obligation of another. The Bible teaches that it's better not to assume surety on a loan. Proverbs 17:18 says "A man lacking in sense pledges and becomes guarantor in the presence of his neighbor."

So how can someone borrow without assuming surety? One

example is with a car loan. Suppose you purchase a car for $15,000 and put $2000 down and sign a note for the remaining $13,000. In essence, you have assumed surety for part of the loan. If you aren't able to make payments on the loan, the car will be repossessed. It can be sold for perhaps $10,000. You will have to make up the difference ($3,000—or less, depending on how many payments you've made).

The obvious way to avoid surety would be to make a larger down payment so the car itself would be the collateral for the loan. If you couldn't make payments, you could surrender the car and cover the note.

> **Americans and debt**
>
> The total amount of household debt in the U.S. is $13.8 trillion.[1]

The Bible also teaches that it's wrong to borrow and not repay. Psalm 37:21 says, "The wicked borrows and does not pay back, but the righteous is gracious and gives."

Doesn't the Bible teach that we should never go into debt?

Some have taught that Christians should never go into debt. The basis for this is usually the passage in Romans 13:8 that says, "Owe nothing to anyone."

Although some have argued that this phrase prohibits debt, it needs to be seen in context. The passage is not a specific teaching about debt but rather a summary of our duty as Christians to governmental authority. Paul is teaching that we shouldn't owe anything to anyone (honor, taxes, and so on). But he isn't teaching that we should never incur debt. While it's better that we are debt-free, this passage isn't commanding us to never go into debt.

The Bible is filled with passages that provide guidelines for lending and borrowing. If debt were always wrong, then these passages wouldn't exist. After all, why have passages providing guidelines for debt if debt is not permitted? Certainly there would be a clear prohibition against it. We should point out that the clear implication of Romans 13:8 is that we should pay our debts and that we're wise if we pay our debts off as quickly as possible.

Let's also acknowledge that some people end up in debt through no fault of their own. They may have been swindled in a business. They may have made a good-faith attempt to start a business but were unsuccessful because their competitors or suppliers cheated them. They may have been unfairly sued in court. The reasons are many.

What are the consequences of debt?

The Bible describes debt as a form of slavery. It's worth repeating what is said in Proverbs 22:7: "The rich rule over the poor, and the borrower is a servant to the lender" (NIV). The borrower becomes a servant (or slave) to the person who is the lender.

> **Debt vs. credit**
>
> In our society, the words *debt* and *credit* are often used interchangeably. To put it simply, *debt* is something that is owed. The Bible does not prohibit borrowing, but it certainly does not recommend it. *Credit* is the establishment of mutual trust between a lender and borrower.

In the Old Testament debt was often connected to slavery. For example, both debts and slavery were cancelled in the years of Jubilee. Sometimes people even put themselves in slavery because of debt (Deuteronomy 15:2,12).

Today we may not be in actual slavery from debt, but it may feel like it sometimes. We have all heard the quip, "I owe, I owe, so off to work I go." If you're deep in debt you know there may be very few days off and perhaps no vacation. Someone in debt can begin to feel like a slave.

How can you know if you're too far in debt? Here are a few questions to ask. Do you have an increasing collection of past-due bills on your desk? Do you drive down the road hoping you'll win the lottery? Do you feel stress every time you think about your finances?

Do you avoid answering the phone because you think it might be a collection agency?

One of the consequences of debt is often a *denial of reality*. In order to realistically deal with the debt in our lives we need to get rid of some of the silly ideas running around in our heads.

For example, you are *not* going to win the lottery. Your debt problem is *not* going to go away if you just ignore it. And a computer glitch in your lender's computer is *not* going to accidentally wipe out your financial records so you don't have to repay your debt.

Another consequence of debt is a *loss of integrity*. When we can't pay, we start saying, "The check's in the mail," when it isn't. We not only kid ourselves, but we try to mislead others about the extent of our problem.

> **An infamous example**
>
> When talking about debt, some commentators refer to "the smiling man on the lawn mower." The word picture comes from a popular TV commercial that showed a man on a riding lawn mower who describes his assets, smiling broadly. He has cars, a home, and a membership in a country club. "How could I afford all these things?" he asks. "Because I'm up to my eyeballs in debt!" He has come to epitomize Americans in debt.

Sometimes debt even leads to dishonesty. As we saw earlier, Psalm 37:21 says, "The wicked borrows and does not pay back." We should repay our debts.

A third consequence of debt is *addiction*. Debt is addictive. Once in debt we begin to get comfortable with cars, consumer goods, furniture, and so on, all funded through debt. Once we reach that comfort level, we go into further debt.

A final consequence of debt is *stress*. Stress experts have calculated the impact of various stress factors on our lives.[2] Some of the greatest are the death of a spouse and divorce. But it's amazing how many other stress factors are financially related (change in financial state, mortgage over $100,000). When we owe more than we can pay, we worry and feel a heavy load of stress that wouldn't exist if we lived debt-free.

What are some common attitudes that lead to debt?

Because so many people are in debt, it's good to begin by identifying why this happens. By understanding some of these attitudes and pressures, we can begin to fend off some of the temptations. Here are three key issues:

1. *Social pressure.* This is the assumption that "everyone's doing it." After all, debt has become a way of life, so most people don't think twice about it. That was not the case a few decades ago, as we've already seen. But even today, a wise and discerning person should seriously question whether going into debt is a good idea.

2. *Ignorance.* Most of us have never had much training in finance and basic economics. So if everyone else is going into debt to get what they want, we assume that debt is the best way to enjoy the good life.

3. *Desire.* Indulgence drives most people today. We assume we need everything right now. Just a couple of generations ago, most material goods were seen as a privilege. Today they've become rights. We think we have the right to a large house, two cars, and the latest electronic gear (TVs, stereos, cell phones). Instead of starting out small and paying as we go, most of us use credit to jump to a lifestyle we really couldn't afford if it weren't for buying with debt and credit.

Credit-card debt

How bad is credit-card debt? To listen to the news reports, you'd think that Americans are drowning in debt. But the story isn't that simple.

The latest economic statistics say that the average U.S. household has more than $9000 in credit-card debt. The average household also spends more than $1300 a year in interest payments for that debt.

While these numbers are true, they're also misleading. The average debt per American household with at least one credit card is $9000. But nearly one-fourth of Americans don't even own credit cards.

Even more telling is the fact that more than 30 percent of American households paid off their most recent credit-card bills in full. So actually a majority of Americans owe nothing to credit-card companies. Of the households that do owe money on credit cards, the median balance was $2200. Only about 1 in 12 American households owes more than $9000.

> ### College debt
>
> Nearly two-thirds (65 percent) of four-year undergraduate students graduate with debt. The average student-loan debt among graduating seniors is over $19,000. One quarter of students borrow $25,000 or more, and one tenth borrow $35,000 or more.[3]

This $9000 figure comes from CardWeb. It takes the outstanding credit-card debt in America and divides it by the number of households that have at least one credit card. While the average is accurate, it's also misleading. Liz Pulliam Weston explains:

> The example I usually give to illustrate the fallacy of averages is to imagine that you and 17 of your friends were having dinner with Bill Gates and Warren Buffett. The average net worth of a person at that table would be about $5 billion. The fact that everybody else's personal net worth was a lot less wouldn't affect the average that much because Bill and Warren are so much wealthier than the rest of us.[4]

Yes, Americans are in debt. And some Americans are *really* in debt. If you're one of those individuals, you should apply the biblical principles we're discussing to your situation. If you aren't, learn a vicarious lesson about what can happen if you don't pay attention to debt.

Here are some principles for dealing with credit-card debt:

- First, *realize that the problem is not the credit card in your hand.* The problem may be with the person holding the credit card. Proverbs 22:3 says, "The prudent sees the evil and hides himself, but the naïve go on, and are punished for it."

- Second, *never use credit cards except for budgeted purchases.* Impulse shopping with credit cards is one of the major reasons people find themselves in debt.

- Third, *pay off your credit cards every month.* If you can't pay off your bill, don't use your card again until you can pay the bill.

  Don't think you are making progress by merely making the minimum payment. When you make only a minimum payment, you're in bondage (Proverbs 22:7). You won't get out of debt this way. At the standard credit-card interest rate, it could take you more than two decades to pay off your debt.

> **Credit cards**
>
> Most Americans carry between 5 and 10 credit cards, but some people carry up to 50 credit cards. According to the *Guinness Book of World Records,* one American has 1,497 credit cards.[5]

- Fourth, *pay your credit card bill on time.* Nearly half of all credit cards issued have a "universal default" clause, which allows the credit-card company to increase the interest rate on your card if you pay a bill more than 30 days late *to another creditor* (even if you pay your bill to them on time).

Should I get rid of credit cards completely?

After reading about all the problems with credit cards, you might be ready to get rid of them. Significant minorities of people don't have them. Some don't because they abused them and therefore discarded them. Others have never applied for credit or don't qualify for it, or they simply don't want the temptation. But that doesn't mean all of us should avoid credit cards.

The problem isn't with credit or credit cards. Their misuse is the problem. If you can't handle credit effectively, it would probably be good to avoid credit cards.

> **Cash or credit?**
>
> A study by Dun and Bradstreet found that on average people spend 12 to 18 percent more when making a purchase with a credit card as opposed to cash.[6]

Credit cards do provide some services you may want to consider. Many purchases are easier with them. If you travel out of state (and especially if you travel out of the country), a credit card is much more useful. It's difficult to write a check when you're out of your local area. And most of us don't want to carry lots of cash.

Some purchases *require* a credit card. Try to rent a car without one. It's often difficult or impossible. Some car-rental agencies will take an ATM card, but most want a credit card.

Finally, a wise use of credit cards can improve your credit rating and build credit in your name. But again, wisdom requires those two basic rules: 1) Pay off your credit card each month. 2) Use credit cards only for budgeted purchases and avoid using them for impulse spending.

What about the debt of a home mortgage?

Most Christian financial counselors put a home mortgage in a different category than other debt. There are a number of reasons for this.

First, *a home loan is secured by the equity in the house*. After an initial down payment, a loan schedule (payment of principal and interest) is applied to the balance of the home expense. If a home-owner faces a financial crisis, he or she can sell the house and use that amount to retire the loan.

Second, *a house is often an appreciating asset.* In many housing markets, the price of a house increases every year. This makes it an even less risky financial investment. But of course, what goes up can also go down. Many homeowners have seen the value of their home decrease significantly. That affects their ability to repay their loan if they need to sell their house.

Third, *a home mortgage is a tax deduction* and thus provides a small financial benefit to homeowners that they wouldn't have if they were renting. At the same time, eager home buyers shouldn't overestimate the value of this and justify buying a home that is beyond their means.

Fourth, *the interest on a home loan is usually within a few percentage points of the prime rate.* This means that the interest rate on a typical home loan is about one third the interest rate of a typical credit card.

While a home mortgage may be different from other forms of debt, that doesn't mean there aren't dangers and pitfalls. As we've already mentioned, people buy houses assuming they'll appreciate in value. But many find that house prices stagnate or even decline. After paying closing costs, they may owe more on their home loan than they receive from the sale of their house.

Another concern about a home mortgage is that many homeowners end up buying more house than they can really afford. Just because they can qualify for a particular loan doesn't mean they should buy a house that will stress them financially.

Also, changing financial circumstances may surprise a couple that has a house mortgage. For example, the wife may get pregnant and no longer be able to work and provide the income necessary to make the monthly payment. Either partner might get laid off from work. And there are always unexpected expenses (new furnace, hot-water heater, and so on) that couples may not have budgeted for when they made their purchase.

One formula that is often used in regard to a home mortgage is to buy a house whose mortgage principle is less than two-and-a-half times a family's annual gross income. Another is to consider what you currently pay in rent and compare that amount to the home mortgage (plus the additional expenses such as insurance, taxes, and so on). The two amounts should be similar.

One other thing to consider with a home mortgage is the length of the loan. If you get a standard 30-year mortgage instead of getting a mortgage for 15 years, you'll end up paying approximately 50 percent more over the lifetime of the loan. Many homeowners who understand this still end up getting a 30-year mortgage but convince themselves they'll pay extra on the loan. The vast majority do not. Get a 15-year mortgage and save yourself lots of money.

Should I get a payday loan?

One of the ways people get themselves in more debt is through payday loans. These are small, short-term loans made by check cashers or similar businesses at high interest rates. Payday lenders provide these loans for people who have "too much month at the end of their paycheck" and need a small loan to get them to their next payday. They write a personal check for the amount they want (plus a fee), and the loan lasts until the next paycheck. The fees for payday loans are extremely high, and this "loan-sharking" explains why a dozen states already ban such loans.

> **Payday loans**
>
> The payday-loan industry argues that high fees are necessary because of the risk they take in giving such loans. But studies have shown that the default rate is really around 2 to 3 percent and thus does not justify the high fees.

Online lenders collect by accessing a person's bank account directly. They also make their money from the exorbitant fees. Although the fee of $15 to $17 per $100 may not seem like too much, it works out to be an annual interest rate in the range of 300 to 500 percent!

Payday loans become a trap. Rarely are they used on a one-time basis, even though that's what is claimed by the industry. One researcher found that the average payday-loan customer makes 11 transactions a year.[7] Most people who borrow using a payday loan are significantly in debt. The high rates make it difficult for most of them to repay the loan. In the end, they find themselves on a perpetual debt treadmill. Jane Bryant Quinn explains: You borrow once and end up short the next month. So you end up borrowing again. Now you are behind once again and have to pay another fee. Over a two-year period, a $300 loan that is renewed again and again will cost $2340 or more. And you're still in debt.[8]

The bottom line is simply this: Payday loans are a bad idea.

Should I get a consolidation loan?

Consolidation loans can be useful because they help you pay off your immediate creditors and then make one payment instead of several. It's very tempting to pursue such a loan, especially when multiple creditors are calling you at home and hounding you for payment. For a disciplined person, a consolidation loan might be the answer.

But the problem is that most people who get into debt do so because they lack the discipline to get out of debt. So a consolidation loan might actually make a difficult financial problem worse by treating the symptom rather than the problem.

It's not uncommon for someone to get a consolidation loan and then, a year later, find themselves owing several new creditors as well as the firm that provided the consolidation loan. If a consolidation loan accompanies a sound financial plan with accountability (sometimes offered by the firm or agency providing the loan), then there's a better chance of success. A consolidation loan isn't the first step. A financial plan (with a reasonable budget) should be the first step toward becoming debt-free.

Should I use my bank's overdraft protection?

Although there's nothing wrong with this service, unfortunately too many people abuse the system and hurt themselves. Human nature is such that quickly we begin to abuse this service and always assume there will be a financial backup for our check-writing irresponsibility.

It reminds me of people who set the clocks in their house 15 minutes ahead so they won't be late. For a few days it works, but quickly everyone in the house simply adjusts to the fact that the clock is 15 minutes fast. Soon they're back to being late.

If you want to have overdraft protection, provide it yourself. The next time you get some unexpected income, deposit it in your account, but don't add it to your check register, and don't add it when you reconcile your bank statement. If you can put $1000 in your account it makes it easy to reconcile each month (just add $1000 to the amount in your checkbook).

I've done this for years and often forget I have an additional $1000 in the checkbook. I've found that my account balances out to around $1000 instead of around $0 each month. Why have the bank provide overdraft protection when you can do it yourself?

How can I build up a good credit rating?

We should all desire to have a good credit rating. Proverbs 22:1 says, "A good name is to be more desired than great wealth, favor is better than silver and gold." We need to work on having a good financial reputation. Frankly, it takes time to build a good reputation—and very little time to ruin it.

It's important that you know your credit score. The FICO score is a three-digit number ranging from 350 to 850, and you should have a score above 660 in order to get the lowest interest rate. Better is a score over 720, which is considered very good. The FICO score is determined by your bill-paying history and your outstanding balances on your credit cards. Various Web sites give you tips on how to improve your credit score, but let's focus instead on what you should *avoid* doing.

We can see how to establish a good credit rating by seeing how easy it is to create a *bad* one. You should do just the opposite if you want to have a good one.

A quick way to obtain a bad credit rating is *failing to pay your bills.* As we've noted, Psalm 37:21 says, "The wicked borrows and does not pay back, but the righteous is gracious and gives." While it should be obvious that we should pay our bills, many people have convinced themselves they don't need to if they don't have the money. However, a lost job or a drop in income is *not* an excuse for not paying your bills.

Maybe you can't pay all your bills. At the very least you need to communicate with your creditors. This means you need to say more than "I can't pay my bills." You need to tell them what you are doing to try to rectify the situation. Have you put together a budget to deal with the situation? Have you contacted a credit bureau? If you want to have a good credit rating, pay your bills and communicate with your creditors if you might have a problem doing so.

Another way to get a bad credit rating is *failing to pay your bills on time.* Ecclesiastes 5:4 says, "When you make a vow to God, do not be late in paying it; for He takes no delight in fools." Delinquent payments and late charges are a quick way to a bad credit rating. If you want to have a good credit rating, pay your bills on time. Pay attention to the due date on every bill, and pay it before it is due (to leave time for it to arrive by mail).

Failing to correct an incorrect credit history is another way to get a bad credit rating. Credit bureaus do make mistakes. Check your credit rating and credit history occasionally to make sure there are no mistakes. If there are mistakes, show the credit bureau through cancelled checks and other receipts what your credit history should actually reflect.

Finally, one way to get a bad credit rating is to *never use credit*. This seems counterintuitive. I've had people tell me that they must have a good credit rating since they've never used credit. They reason that since they have never misused credit, they must have a good rating.

This is not so. If you don't have a credit history, you can't have a good credit rating. If you want to establish a good credit history, you need to demonstrate that you can use credit responsibly.

Should a Christian ever file for bankruptcy?

Since Christians file for bankruptcy every year, the real question is whether it's scriptural to do so. There's no verse in the Bible that says, "Thou shall not file for bankruptcy." But there are key biblical principles that do apply to this question.

What can I do if I'm being hounded by creditors?

The obvious way to avoid being hounded is to not misuse credit and go into debt. A legitimate business deserves to be paid and certainly has a right to ask when they will be paid.

But some creditors cross the line and harass people who owe them money. In those cases, it's important to know that the 1986 Consumer Protection Act gives you some relief from hounding. The act prohibits such things as phone calls very early in the morning or late at night. It also prohibits calls to you at your place of employment if your employer disapproves. If a creditor violates these provisions in the Consumer Protection Act, you can gain relief by contacting the Federal Trade Commission.

First, the Bible teaches that we should repay what we owe. Ecclesiastes 5:5 says, "It is better that you should not vow than that you should vow and not pay." When you used credit to make purchases or pay for services, did you promise to pay? You may not have actually said the words, "I promise to pay you back." But you essentially have made a vow to repay the debt.

Second, as noted earlier, some people are forced into bankruptcy through no fault of their own. A worker stole from their business or an officer of the company embezzled funds. They may have been in a car accident or had a major medical expense (surgery, rehabilitation) and can't get insurance to pay the bills. There are lots of examples of this. The government does allow for bankruptcy, and we are to obey government (Romans 13:1-7).

How can someone get out of debt?

The best way to deal with debt is to never get into it in the first place. But if you're already in debt, you need to break the cycle with discipline applied over time. Here are the steps:

1. *Establish the right priorities.* God owns it all (Job 41:11; Psalm 24:1). Unfortunately, we often believe that *we* own it all. We need to mentally transfer ownership of all our possessions to God (Psalm 8). This also includes giving the Lord His part and honoring Him with your giving (even if it is a small amount).

2. *Stop borrowing.* If a pipe breaks in your house, the first thing you do is shut off the water, before you start to mop it up. Before you do anything else, "shut off" the borrowing. Don't use your credit card. Don't take out a bank loan.

3. *Develop a budget.* This is something you can do by yourself or—better for many people—with the help of online ministries and financial services that provides guidelines. Or you can consult with a financial expert who can give you guidelines.

    You begin by making a list of all of your monthly expenses (mortgage or rent, utilities, groceries, car payments, credit-card bills, and so on). Then you need to establish a priority for the outstanding loans you have. This should include information about the amount owed and the interest rates. Then you need to set a realistic budget that allows you to have enough money to pay off the loans in a systematic way.

Write to each creditor with a repayment plan based upon this realistic budget. It might even be good to include a financial statement and a copy of your budget so they can see you're serious about paying the money you owe them.

4. *Begin to retire your debt.* If you can, pay extra on the debts with the highest interest rates. If all of them have comparable interest rates, you might instead pay extra on the one with the smallest balance. By paying that off first, you'll have a feeling of accomplishment and then free up some of your income to tackle your next debt.

5. *Develop new spending habits.* For example, if you generate extra income from working overtime or at an extra job, use that to retire your debt faster. Don't assume that because you have some extra income you can spend it on yourself.

Before you buy anything, question yourself. If an item isn't in your budget, ask yourself if you really need it and how much use you'll get out of it. We often spend because we're used to spending. Change your spending habits.

∼

As we've already mentioned, debt is like a form of slavery. Do what you can to be debt-free. If you follow these steps faithfully, that can take place in a few years. Debt freedom will reduce your stress and free you up to accomplish what God intends for you to do.

5

Saving *and* Investing

Getting out of debt is an important goal. However, we should desire to do more than just break even. Saving and investing should be part of our budget and part of our life plan. Ultimately, they're a means to an end. We may be saving for our kids' college or saving for our retirement.

But in order to save, we need to deal with the materialism and consumerism we discussed earlier. We have to get off the consumption treadmill if we are to have the financial resources to save and invest. We must free ourselves from giving in to the temptations to spend more than we earn. Only in that way will we have financial freedom.

We used to be a nation of savers. In fact, thrift was a foundational element of American society. The architect Louis Sullivan even carved the word *thrift* over the door of his bank. Thrift was seen as a private moral virtue that made public prosperity possible. Americans supported institutions that encouraged savings. These "pro-thrift institutions also limited the amount of debt consumers could carry," and "some forms of thriftlessness were outlawed entirely" such as lotteries and usury.[1]

Unfortunately, thrift died a few decades ago. David Tucker says that after the Great Depression, economists began to portray thrift as a vice that "threw sand in the gears of our consumer economy."[2]

Today, Americans save less than ever. Personal savings as a percentage of disposable income were around 10 percent in the 1980s. They hovered around 5 percent during much of the 1990s. By 2000 they neared zero percent and have sometimes dropped below zero.

Obviously we need to be saving, but there may be different reasons for doing so. It's therefore important to understand the different ways you'll want to save and invest. Some saving will be short-term saving. This includes setting aside money in an emergency fund. As we'll discuss in a moment, this is essential and should be your first goal in saving. But it also makes sense to have enough in your savings to cover some unexpected and necessary purchases.

> **Americans and saving**
>
> One survey found that more than half of Americans (52 percent) said they aren't saving adequately. And 17 percent said they can't afford to save at all! And the survey also found that, while 35 percent are saving, they're not saving enough to meet their short-term and long-term financial needs.[3]

By contrast, other saving and investing may be more long-term. This includes setting aside money for your children's college fund or providing for your retirement. In this case, liquidity is less important and long-term performance is more important. At first these may be such things as government securities. Later your investment portfolio might include such things as stocks, bonds, and balanced mutual funds.

The Bible and saving

The Bible encourages us to save. In Proverbs it encourages those who don't save to consider how a lowly creature like the ant prepares for the future:

> Go to the ant, you sluggard; consider its ways and be wise!
> It has no commander, no overseer or ruler, yet it stores its provisions in summer and gathers its food at harvest (Proverbs 6:6-8 NIV).

The writer of Proverbs also talks about how wise people save, in contrast to foolish people who don't: "In the house of the wise are stores of choice food and oil, but a foolish man devours all he has" (Proverbs 21:20 NIV).

We should always have a budget. Author and speaker John Maxwell has a great definition: "A budget is people telling their money what to do instead of wondering where it went." A budget is a plan for saving and spending. The book of Proverbs admonishes us to plan. Proverbs 16:3 says, "Commit your works to the LORD and your plans will be established." But as we develop these plans for the future, we also need to be sensitive to the Lord's leading. "The mind of man plans his way, but the LORD directs his steps" (Proverbs 16:9).

The Bible says that good things will happen when we plan. "Good planning and hard work lead to prosperity" (Proverbs 21:5 NLT). By contrast, the Bible also teaches that our plans will fail if these plans aren't within the will of God. Isaiah 30:1 says, "You make plans that are contrary to mine" (NLT).

If you don't have anything in savings, you need to begin by putting aside a cash reserve for emergencies. Proverbs 22:5 says, "A prudent person foresees danger and takes precautions. The simpleton goes blindly on and suffers the consequences" (NLT). Everyone needs a cash reserve for major emergencies (fire, tornado, earthquake) and even for small emergencies and inconveniences (a broken appliance, car repair, a flat tire).

Most financial advisors suggest that you have six months' worth of income set aside for an emergency or unexpected expense. You may not have that set aside right now, but today is a good time to start. Perhaps your first goal would be to set aside one or two months' worth of income.

What should I know about banking?

Most of us grew up around banks and have a fairly good idea of what they do and what services they offer. Although some people avoid banks and the modern banking system, there is nothing unbiblical or immoral about using the services of a bank. But you should be aware of the strengths, weaknesses, and limitations of banking.

A bank is a safe place to put your money. Your deposits are insured for at least $250,000 (sometimes more depending on how your accounts are structured) by the Federal Deposit Insurance Corporation (www.fdic.gov). Banks provide lots of services that you may want to use. More and more people use online banking, and most people have an ATM card or debit card. Generally the interest a bank pays on savings accounts is much lower than you can find elsewhere. In fact, the inflation rate is usually higher than the interest a bank will pay on an account, so you're actually losing money over time.

What about the various services a bank offers? In our previous chapter on debt and credit, we found that the problem isn't so much with the credit card as with the person using the card. This is also true of various banking services, such as ATM cards, debit cards, payroll deductions, and automatic debit. All have their place, but we should make sure we have a budget and the discipline to use them correctly.

ATM cards provide the user with access to cash 24 hours a day. But there are some concerns and limitations:

1. Make sure you keep an accurate record of the amounts you withdraw, and don't forget to include any additional charges that will be added to your account. Frequent trips to an ATM machine that adds additional charges to your account can turn out to be more expensive than going to the bank and writing a check for cash.

2. Don't depend on the ATM to give you an accurate balance for your checking account. There may be additional checks that haven't cleared your bank and won't show up on the balance provided by the ATM.

3. If you lose your card, report it immediately. Someone may be withdrawing funds from your account!

Debit cards are accepted like credit cards but function more like ATM cards. Purchases you make in a store are automatically deducted from your checking account. Use it the way you would use a check, but make sure you enter the transaction in your check register.

Many people use banking services to take care of their paycheck and their payroll deductions. *Direct deposit* permits the employer to directly deposit your paycheck into your bank account. While convenient, it may have some limitations. You still need to check and make sure that the bank received the check and that it was deposited in the proper account. If your employer or the bank makes a mistake, you could be writing checks on an account with insufficient funds and end up bouncing checks.

Payroll deductions allow employers to deduct certain amounts for benefits you designate. These deductions are typically for taxes (federal, state, and local) and entitlement programs (Social Security, Medicare). Other deductions can be for various benefits like insurance and retirement. Although they're convenient, it's still important to confirm that the amounts are being deducted.

When you use automatic debit payment, you can be relatively sure that your payment for a service will be credited on the payment due date. Your bank is supposed to pay the bill on the designated date each month. While this

> **ATMs can be expensive**
>
> A survey by Bankrate .com found that the average ATM fee your bank will charge when you use another institution's ATM is $1.25. And that is on top of the average fee of $1.78 that other institution will charge you for using their ATM machine.

is convenient, it's still important to make sure your bill was paid to the proper account. When you receive the next month's statement, you should check and make sure that it was paid correctly.

As we mentioned in the chapter on giving, many Christians now give through an automatic deduction from their checking account. While this has the positive effect of providing regular support for a church or Christian organization, we shouldn't forget to pray for the ministry even though we aren't writing a monthly check to it.

Banks also offer overdraft protection. This is a valuable service to have, especially when the bank or the employer makes a mistake. But it can also be abused as mentioned in the previous chapter.

Before you open an account at a bank and begin to select services, you would be wise to shop for bank services on the Internet. You can compare fees, deposit requirements, and services of various banks before you walk in the door. Instead of a bank, you might also consider going to a financial institution that offers bank services (credit union accounts, mutual funds, money market funds, and so on). Comparing services before you walk into a bank or other financial institution is the best way to find what's best for you.

Basic principles concerning investing

Whether you're a beginning investor or someone who has been at it a long time, there are some investment basics that will make your life easier and substantially reduce your stress.

1. *Pick investments that are easy to understand and track.* The more complicated an investment, the less likely you are to understand what is taking place and certainly the less likely you are to track its progress. If an investment advisor starts talking to you about derivatives or leveraged deals and you're confused, it's probably time for you to leave. If you don't understand an investment on the front end, it's unlikely you'll understand it later on.

2. *Invest with a goal in mind.* Is this investment for your kid's college? Is it for your retirement? When you have a clear goal (and deadline) this will be helpful in picking your investment in regard to its risk and rate of return.

3. *Set a budget for investing.* Some people spend too much on investing, but most spend too little or nothing at all. If you don't set aside something to invest each month, you probably won't invest anything at all.

4. *Never take on an investment that causes you or your family too much stress.* If you're always worrying about your investment, you probably have the wrong one. Avoid "get rich quick" schemes. Avoid personal liability, and avoid surety in an investment.

5. *Prepare for the unexpected.* What if you need the money in your investment earlier than you planned? Is there a penalty? What is the penalty? Does the investment have liquidity? We should never plan on everything in our lives going smoothly. Murphy's Law is still in effect. (And as the joke goes, Murphy was an optimist.)

6. *Diversify your investments.* We all have heard the phrase, "Put all your eggs in one basket, and watch that basket." That may be true about some things, but it's bad investment advice. We've probably all heard of people who invested most or all of their funds in one company or one market sector. For a time these investments might do well, but eventually a company or business sector declines or even fails. I heard of one man who invested heavily in the technology sector in the 1990s. He did well until the dot-com collapse and then had substantial losses.

Solomon gives excellent investment advice: "Divide your portion to seven, or even to eight, for you do not know what misfortune may occur on the earth" (Ecclesiastes 11:2). It makes sense to diversify your portfolio since no human being can accurately and consistently predict the future (James 4:13-15). By diversifying your investments, you minimize the risk to your entire portfolio.

7. *Put some of your investments in gold.* Investing in metals (like gold and silver) makes sense. Returns from gold help offset losses from other assets (such as stocks). Gold has also been a good hedge against inflation. In the last chapter of this book, we talk about government debt as well as its unfunded liabilities. It is likely that the government will have to print money, and that will lead to inflation.

When you invest in other market sectors in a time of inflation, you are being paid back in devalued dollars. Gold maintains value as the value of the dollar declines. A wise and discerning investor will consider which investments make sense in an economy where inflation and a devalued dollar exist.

8. *Consider the morality of your investments.* Although investing is a legitimate activity, many Christians and Christian groups have begun to pay attention to *where* their money is invested. Certain values-based investing groups monitor various funds to make sure these investments aren't being used to promote abortion, pornography, gambling, or homosexuality. Christians are admonished to have nothing to do with "the unfruitful deeds of darkness" (Ephesians 5:11). Paying attention to where our investment goes is one way to obey this command.

9. *Seek godly wisdom.* When investing, make sure you consult with others who know more about it. Many of the Proverbs admonish us to seek wise counsel:

- Proverbs 15:22: "Plans fail for lack of counsel, but with many advisers they succeed" (NIV).

- Proverbs 19:20: "Listen to counsel and accept discipline, that you may be wise the rest of your days."

- Proverbs 12:15: "The way of a fool is right in his own eyes, but a wise man is he who listens to counsel."

How should I maintain my investments?

Before you invest, make sure you take time to make wise decisions. Sadly, most of us take more time doing research on which car to buy than we spend doing research on investments. We probably put more trust in an investment advisor than in a car salesman. We should get investment advice, but we also need to do some research on our own.

You should also take time to review your investment portfolio. You may have made a wise decision about your asset allocation (stocks, bonds, and so on), but circumstances change. More likely,

> **Make sure you get all that's coming to you**
>
> If your company offers a match for your retirement contributions (401-k and so on), then make sure you're participating. If they provide a full match, then you're doubling your investment each month. Even if they match at a lower percentage, this is a company benefit you don't want to ignore.

you made some good choices and some bad choices. Take time to review what choices you made and change your investment portfolio appropriately.

Then, invest regularly. This principle is related to the previous one. We need to see investing as a process, not just a one-time event. Moreover, it needs to be done regularly, just like paying bills. Often we pay our bills and think of investing as only a last resort. At the end of each year, make sure you've fully funded your IRA.

What are some myths about retirement?

One principle reason for investing is to save money for retirement. But sadly, many people doing this make certain assumptions because of prevailing myths surrounding retirement. What are these myths, and what is the true reality?

1. *I don't know if I'll live that long, so I don't need to save that much for retirement.* While this may have been true a few decades ago, it's no longer true for the average American.

The fact is, you'll probably live 20 years or more in retirement. And if you're a woman, you'll probably live longer than that.

When Social Security was implemented in the 1930s, the average American was living to age 63. You didn't receive benefits until you were age 65. Now, more than eight out of every ten Americans zoom past the age of 65. You'd better be ready to live longer, and you'd better have money set aside to do so.

2. *Social Security will cover most of my retirement expenses.* This myth is beginning to give way to reality. Surveys show that the younger you are, the more likely you are to believe that Social Security won't be there for you when you retire. Years ago, the ratio between workers and beneficiaries used to be 20-to-1. Then it fell to 10-to-1, then 5-to-1. By the middle of this century, it will be closer to 2-to-1. Also, Social Security is one of those unfunded government liabilities that's certain to change significantly in the future because there are not enough financial reserves available to the federal government.

While most people recognize that Social Security won't cover all their expenses, they do expect it to cover most of them. That is a big mistake. For example, the more money you earn while you're working, the less income (as a percentage) your Social Security payments will cover.

3. *If Social Security isn't going to be there for me in the future, I might as well retire early and get my benefits now.* But if you begin to take Social Security early (say at age 62), you won't get your full benefits later. Unless you're disabled, taking early retirement could reduce your benefits by up to 25 percent. And even if you decide to retire early, you won't receive Medicare benefits until you're 65.

Consider what will happen if you wait to retire. For example, if you wait until age 68 or even age 70, you'll actually be increasing your benefits *substantially* for the rest of your life. Go to the government Web site for Social Security (www.ssa.gov) to see the impact of retiring later in life.

4. *I won't need as much money to live when I retire.* Most people believe they'll spend less in retirement (most people estimate 20 percent less). While that may be true for some people (don't have to commute to work, buy professional-looking clothes for work, buy business lunches, and so on), the reality is that we often get accustomed to a lifestyle and carry that same lifestyle into retirement. For many couples retirement means travel. In those cases, retirement might even be more expensive.

5. *I have money set aside in a retirement fund and don't need to be concerned about inflation.* Already inflation has been eating away at your savings even when it has been at a relatively low percentage. Just wait until the government (through the Federal Reserve) begins to print more money in order to meet the demands of various entitlement programs as well as financial bailouts. The money you set aside will be worth even less in the future.

〜

Saving and investing are an important part of wise money management. None of us are born knowing how to manage money. That's why we need to learn these principles and apply them with wisdom to our situation. Learn the principles, create a savings and investment plan, and stick to your plan. That's the best path to financial success.

We don't have any guarantee that we'll always make lots of money from our investments. The only sure guarantee is that we'll have no financial security if we sit back and do nothing. Now is the time to learn, establish a budget, and begin to save and invest.

6

Insurance

Should I have insurance? The answer to that question is an unequivocal *yes*. Many financial planners consider life insurance to be a cornerstone of sound financial management. And other forms of insurance (such as car insurance and home insurance) are mandated by government. In this chapter we'll look at the various types of insurance that should be part of our financial planning.

Life insurance

Some Christians wonder whether life insurance is biblical. After all, if I'm trusting in God, why should I have life insurance?

Insurance is not actually mentioned in the Bible, but there are many biblical passages that speak of planning for the future (Isaiah 32:8; Proverbs 16:9). It isn't a lack of faith to own life insurance (or even other forms of insurance). We can trust in God and yet still own insurance that will provide for our family in case of death or disability. But we should be careful not to transfer our trust from God to insurance.

What are some of the reasons to have life insurance? First, it can *provide the funds necessary to pay for your funeral and burial costs*. And if you suffer from a lingering illness, life insurance can help pay for medical expenses and other debts you may incur before your death.

Another important function of life insurance is to *provide replacement income.* If your family relies on your income for support, that income stops with your death. While this may be obvious to someone with a young family, it's also true of couples with older children or even an empty nest. We may not realize how much even a dual-income family depends upon one person's income until it's no longer available. In some cases, government benefits or even employer benefits may be reduced after your death. Life insurance can help make up that gap in income.

A third benefit of life insurance is to *pay for costs of probate.* These legal costs as well as death taxes and other liens can be covered by a life-insurance policy. Often, these costs shock families who don't expect that such large amounts will be levied upon death.

And life insurance can be a way to *create an inheritance for your family.* Although it makes more financial sense to buy term insurance, some families decide to buy a policy that builds cash value. This type of "forced savings" guarantees that there are at least some savings and a small inheritance to your beneficiaries. Moreover, the interest credited is tax deferred and would even be tax exempt if paid as a death claim.

How much life insurance do I need?

It's advisable to consult with an insurance agent before you make a decision about how much life insurance to purchase. Here are a few basic principles to consider.

> **The 5 percent guideline**
>
> Financial planners suggest that insurance account for no more than 5 percent of a family's net spendable income. This estimate doesn't include car or home insurance (and assumes the family has health insurance from an employer).

A good rule of thumb is to determine how much money your family would need in the event of the death of the primary wage earner. Then take that annual amount and multiply it by at least 12. For example, if your annual income was $60,000, you multiply it by 12 to get the amount of $720,000. That would mean you would probably want to purchase life insurance for at least three-quarters of a million dollars. This of course, would be a minimum amount, and you might want to purchase a million-dollar policy. If this money were invested by your beneficiaries at a reasonable rate of return, it would probably provide the necessary income per year for your family.

What kind of life insurance do I need?

You should consult an agent before deciding what kind of life insurance to purchase. But many financial consultants recommend 20-year term insurance that is at least ten times your annual income.

Term insurance is easy to understand. You buy a policy for a fixed period of time (10 years, 20 years). You can choose for your premium to increase each year or for it to be the same amount for a fixed number of years. Term insurance doesn't build any cash value but merely insures you for the term of the policy. Your beneficiaries collect only if you die. If you live past the length of the policy, then neither you nor your family receives any money.

By contrast, permanent life policies not only offer death benefits but also provide a mechanism for savings through what is called "cash value." That means that if you live, you get back a small portion of the amount you spent on your premium. This is obtained by either cashing in the policy or by borrowing against it.

As you would expect, permanent life-insurance premiums are higher than term premiums since some of the premium payment is put into a savings program. One of the reasons many financial planners do not recommend these policies is that the return on investment is low. They believe that most people are better off purchasing a term policy and putting the amount they save into an investment with a better financial return.

There are a number of types of permanent life insurance. First is what is called "traditional whole life." The annual premium is guaranteed, and there are also guaranteed cash values and death benefits.

If you are a conservative investor and want some form of "forced savings," this is a policy to consider.

A second type of policy is "universal life." This policy provides more flexibility in premiums. Premiums can vary from year to year and even be skipped. And a third type of policy is "variable life." This type of policy has the fewest guarantees and allows the policy holder to invest in various funds. While there are guaranteed annual premiums and death benefits, there is no guaranteed cash value since the policyholder may be invested in various (potentially higher risk) funds.

Once again, we should mention that life insurance shouldn't be considered an investment. A significant portion of your premiums are used to buy death-benefit coverage. That's why financial planners suggest that most people buy a term policy and invest the savings from buying it, rather than purchasing a permanent life policy. While the latter does, as mentioned, provide a mechanism for "forced savings," it doesn't provide the best return on investment.

Inheritance

A topic related to life insurance is inheritance. Is inheritance biblical? Certainly it is. The Old Testament provides guidelines for inheritance (Numbers 27; Deuteronomy 21). And the Bible instructs us to pass on an inheritance: "A good man leaves an inheritance to his children's children, and the wealth of the sinner is stored up for the righteous" (Proverbs 13:22).

The New Testament also teaches that we should provide for our families.

> If anyone does not provide for his own, and especially for those of his household, he has denied the faith and is worse than an unbeliever (1 Timothy 5:8).

Not only should a husband provide for his family in life, but also in death. This includes life insurance and a will.

We are currently in the midst of the largest transfer of wealth in history as the "builder" generation passes its wealth on to the baby-boomer generation. And in the next few years, baby boomers will start passing their wealth on to the "buster" generation.

Although passing your inheritance on to your children is biblical, there are certain concerns that many financial planners have noted—the same ones that many of us have seen. When young people inherit a great deal of wealth, it often affects them in negative ways. They become less responsible. They are often tempted to stop working and start spending.

History is full of stories of heirs and heiresses who squandered the millions they inherited. Rarely do we see a legacy of inherited wealth that lasts for more than one or two generations. But you don't have to look back into history to see this. The tabloids have contemporary stories of children born into wealth who are now spending their money like the prodigal son (see Luke 15).

Auto insurance

If you drive a car, you need auto insurance. This isn't an option but a legal necessity. Auto insurance protects you in case you're involved in an accident (whether your fault or not) and also protects you if your car is stolen.

Auto insurance essentially is a contract between you and the insurance company. You pay the premium, and the insurance company agrees to pay for losses as they're defined in your policy. A typical policy is usually for six months and is separated into six different types of coverage. Most states require that you buy some (but not all) of these coverages. And if you're financing the car, your bank or lender may even have certain requirements. These are the six areas of coverage:

1. *Collision*. This coverage pays for any damages to your car resulting from a collision with another vehicle. Collision

coverage is sold with a deductible that may range from $250 to $1000. Here is the key: the higher your deductible, the lower your insurance premium. Seriously consider getting a high deductible. You want insurance to cover what you can't cover with your monthly income. If you have a high deductible, you'll save in the long run with lower insurance premiums.

Collision coverage will reimburse you for the costs of repairing your car, minus the deductible. If you're in an accident where you aren't at fault, your auto insurance company may try to recover the amount they paid you from the other driver's insurance company and possibly reimburse you for the deductible.

2. *Comprehensive.* This coverage reimburses you for loss due to things other than collision. That might include the theft of your car or damage to your car caused by natural disaster (fire, hail, tornado, earthquake) or from falling objects or vandalism. Comprehensive insurance is also sold with a deductible (usually of a few hundred dollars). Again, you may want to opt for a higher deductible as a way of lowering your insurance premium.

3. *Uninsured and underinsured motorist coverage.* This coverage has always been important but is especially necessary today since there are many drivers on the road who don't have auto insurance. This coverage will reimburse you, a member of your family, or even a designated driver if someone driving your car is hit by an uninsured or hit-and-run driver. Underinsured motorist coverage also can be used when a driver who is at fault has insufficient insurance to pay for any loss you sustained in a car accident. This coverage will also protect you if you're hit as a pedestrian.

4. *Bodily injury liability.* This coverage applies to bodily injuries that you (or others driving your car) cause to someone else. This also covers you when you are driving someone else's car with their permission.

   Don't neglect this coverage. If you're involved in a serious car accident, you could be sued for an amount far beyond your ability to pay. It's worthwhile to consider buying more than the minimum required by the state in order to protect your home and your life savings.

5. *Medical payments or personal injury protection*—This coverage pays for the medical cost you and your passengers incur when in an accident. The personal injury protection (PIP) portion can cover a number of things, including medical payments, lost wages, and even the costs associated with replacing some of the services usually rendered by someone who was injured in an auto accident. PIP may also cover funeral costs.

6. *Property damage liability*—This coverage pays for damage you (or someone driving your car with your permission) may cause to someone else's property. This certainly includes damage to another person's car. It also includes damage to a tree, fence, building, or other structure.

Do I need additional insurance to rent a car?

There is no simple answer to that question, given the variables of different auto-insurance policies, various car-rental companies, and various state laws and requirements. The best thing to do is to make two phone calls. .

First, *call your auto insurance company.* Have them explain the coverage you currently have on your car, and find out how that would apply when you rent another car. For example, if you do not have comprehensive on your car, you may not be covered if your rental car is stolen or damaged. Also check to see if there's coverage for towing charges and other expenses you might have to pay for a rental car.

Second, *call your credit-card company.* Many times credit-card companies offer insurance benefits to the cardholder. Usually they cover damage to or loss of a rental car, but check to make sure how much coverage they may provide.

Then when you're at the rental-car counter, have the representatives explain what may or may not be covered. They may offer liability insurance, personal accident insurance, personal-effects coverage, and loss damage waiver (LDW). Be sure you understand your coverages and liabilities before you rent your car.

Home insurance

If you purchase a house, you need home insurance. The lender will require it. Even if you purchase a home without a loan, you still should have insurance.

Usually you'll be purchasing enough to cover the cost of rebuilding your home (but not including the cost of the land). You shouldn't base your cost on the price you paid for your home but rather the cost of rebuilding your house at current construction costs. You can calculate this by multiplying the square footage of your home by local building costs per square foot.

Accounting for inflation

Many policies have an inflation guard. This will automatically adjust the coverage to more accurately reflect current construction costs in your area.

You may also want to consider buying a bit more insurance than the amount you calculate. For example, after a major disaster (flood, tornado, hurricane, earthquake), the rebuilding costs may significantly increase. The cost of building materials will increase, and construction workers will be in greater demand. This can raise the cost of rebuilding substantially.

What are some ways to lower your home-insurance premiums?

The first is to *comparison-shop*. The difference between policies and coverages is often significant. If you have a good credit history and a good claims history, you may find that another insurance company will give you a better deal than what you have in your current policy.

Another way to reduce the cost of your policy is to *raise your deductible*. Just as raising the deductible in your auto insurance can lower your premium, so can raising the deductible on your homeowner's policy. A policy that replaces windows or roof shingles may seem like a good deal when the insurance company sends you a check, but it has cost you plenty in higher premiums.

Another way to lower your premiums is to *make cost-effective improvements* to your home. If you get a home security system, you can lower your premiums. If it is monitored, and thus connected to the police station and fire station, you can save even more. If you have smoke and fire detectors, you can save. If you put on a roof with flame-retardant material, you can save. These and other improvements can save you money.

You can often also save if you *buy your home and automobile insurance from the same company*. If you buy multiple policies, the company will take off a percentage (from 5 to 15 percent) from your premiums. Also, ask about group coverage. Sometimes a professional organization or alumni organization will offer discounts for members of the association.

Health-insurance policies

Medical insurance is important. Many people file for bankruptcy because they're unable to pay for medical expenses. That is why it's crucial to do what you can to obtain and maintain medical insurance.

How to get health insurance has not only been a personal and family decision, but it has also become a public-policy issue. Since most health-insurance benefits are provided through businesses, government regulation has naturally followed. It may surprise you to know that this wasn't always the case.

After World War II, companies began to provide health-care benefits to their employees as an incentive. Soon Americans came to expect that the company they worked for would provide health insurance. If you think about it, this is a bit odd. The company you work for doesn't own your car-insurance policy. It doesn't own your house-insurance policy. But it does own your health-insurance policy. And because it does, government officials regulate it in ways that interrupt natural market forces.

Families and individuals need some form of health insurance. Health-care costs have been increasing every year, usually at twice the rate of inflation. And there's no end in sight for the increase.

A catastrophic illness can destroy a family's finances, and even a series of small health setbacks can disrupt things. A trip to the emergency room can bust a budget, and an extended stay in the hospital can send a family hurtling toward bankruptcy.

The only reasonable answer is adequate health insurance. This is about the only way to avoid the risk of financial disaster from a costly illness or accident. Moreover, a policy that emphasizes preventive health can provide families with professional medical care that can decrease the chance of certain illnesses.

What sort of policy and what kind of coverage should an individual or family have? Answering that question is difficult for two reasons. 1) Businesses often provide a standard policy, and so individuals and families sometimes have very little choice. Fortunately, many businesses are now providing a cafeteria plan which allows individuals and families to choose options that best fit their needs. 2) There are hundreds of different policies with various features. There simply is no "one-size-fits-all" policy for everyone.

Even though there are hundreds of types of policies, they can be broken down into five categories. These are a basic policy for *hospital coverage;* a policy for *surgical expenses;* a policy for *regular medical expenses;* a policy for *major medical expenses;* and a policy for *comprehensive medical expenses.* Many policies include more than one of these categories.

- *Basic hospital coverage.* This kind of policy will usually cover the charges for a hospital room as well as additional expenses (for example, ambulance, emergency room, medical tests, lab fees, and so on). The policy will have certain deductibles and even some exclusions. And it will usually provide benefits that are limited to a certain amount and to a specified number of days in the hospital.

- *Surgical expense coverage.* These policies cover surgical expenses as well as office visits before and after the surgical procedure. The policies will have a schedule of fees as well as a maximum payment for any specified surgical procedure. Usually the policies will also cover the services of a second surgeon and an anesthesiologist. They may also be purchased in conjunction with a hospital policy.

- *Regular medical coverage.* This type of policy will usually provide coverage for services from a physician as well as such things as co-payments (for doctor visits as well as for medicine) and various diagnostic and laboratory tests.

  A typical policy will specify a maximum amount that will be reimbursed and include stipulations concerning deductibles and co-payments. Often regular medical insurance coverage is purchased along with a policy for hospital expense and surgical expense coverage.

- *Major medical coverage.* More and more families and individuals are getting major medical coverage. This kind of policy is designed to cover the massive expenses that occur due to a catastrophic or prolonged illness or an accident. Usually the policy covers hospital, surgical, doctor, and other medical treatment that is not already covered by other types of policies.

A typical major medical policy has a large deductible as well as a co-insurance provision. It might require the insured individual to pay a percentage of the claim. It might also have what is called a "stop-loss" provision, which sets a maximum amount the insured individual has to pay.

If you can't afford a typical health-insurance policy, it's worth investigating a major medical policy. It might have a high deductible and low premium and provide at least some coverage in the event of a major illness or accident.

• *Comprehensive medical coverage.* Some individuals and families opt for a comprehensive medical plan. The policy is just what the name implies. These policies combine the features of the plans previously discussed (basic as well as major medical coverage). Like the other plans, comprehensive will have a co-insurance provision and a deductible clause. As with the other plans, the higher the deductible, the lower the monthly premiums.

Should someone get an individual policy or a group policy?

If you're asking this question, your employer probably does not offer a group policy, or else you are self-employed. But there are still some people who have a choice. Should they get an individual medical policy or a group policy? A significant number of small businesses don't offer health insurance to their employees or else provide it as an optional benefit.

It's true, in general, that premiums for a group policy are lower than those for individual coverage. But it makes sense to comparison-shop and see if that's the case. Make sure you do a true "apples-to-apples" comparison. Sometimes an employer will be paying part of the premium for the policy, so you need to make sure you factor that information into your comparison.

Also, sometimes similar individual policies from different insurance companies can differ by hundreds of dollars. So it's worth shopping around for health insurance.

What about managed-care plans?

Since the 1970s, there has been a significant growth in what have been called "managed-care health-care plans." They work by cutting costs with physicians and hospitals. These costs are cut by negotiating with the involved parties for a reduced charge for their services.

The best known are health maintenance organizations (HMOs). They actually negotiate with employers to administer the insurance details of the health needs of the employees within a company. A major requirement of an HMO is that the patient use the HMO's network of doctors, hospitals, and clinics. Most HMOs also require a co-payment of some sort.

Another form of managed care is a Preferred Provider Organization (PPO). In many ways, a PPO is similar to an HMO. The principal difference is that the patient in a PPO can usually choose the physician they want to see. If a patient goes to a member physician or hospital, the patient's out-of-pocket expenses will be less than if he or she chooses a nonmember provider. A patient is free to choose, but there's a difference in cost depending on whether he or she picks a member or nonmember provider.

One other form of managed care is Point of Service (POS). This

Are you an exception?

In some cases, an individual health-insurance policy may be cheaper. Health insurance is based upon the characteristics of those being insured. It is possible that, if they differ significantly from the characteristics of the group, your demographics (age, sex) and physical condition might make you eligible for an individual policy that's cheaper than the group policy.

plan allows an insured employee to choose his or her primary physician. The insured employee then is supposed to see this physician first for all medical needs. If, however, the insured employee decides to see a specialist first, the out-of-pocket expenses will be greater.

What about other medical plans?

There are many other forms of medical insurance as well as supplemental insurance. Many businesses and individuals carry long-term disability insurance. Some carry accidental death and dismemberment insurance. Sometimes these are part of a comprehensive insurance policy. Sometimes they aren't.

People advanced in years will often get a Medicare supplement, or insurance for long-term elderly care. Medicare is available for most people who are over 65 years of age and for some disabled people. Medicare provides coverage in three parts:

- *Medicare Part A* covers hospital stays. It provides hospital benefits for short-term illness or benefits for nursing facility or home.

- *Medicare Part B* is optional medical insurance and covers doctor visits and pays for most medical and surgical fees

- *Medicare Part D* was recently added as a drug benefit.

A Medicare supplemental insurance plan is designed to pick up the difference between your bill and the actual Medicare payment. It is a relatively inexpensive insurance for the amount of coverage it provides, which usually includes the whole range of health problems.

Medicaid pays medical bills for low-income people who usually cannot afford the cost of medical care. Medicaid and S-CHIP (for children) are government programs that have guidelines for eligibility.

If you lose your job or are laid off by your company, you have some options. A company must give you the option of continuing coverage through COBRA (Consolidated Omnibus Budget Reconciliation Act of 1986). Medical coverage through COBRA is almost always less expensive than what you would pay for individual health coverage. This will usually provide coverage for 18 months.

~

Buying insurance and keeping up to date with insurance policies isn't something most people enjoy. But insurance is necessary, and we can save lots of money by making wise decisions about the various policies we purchase. Following some of the principles described here can save you money and stress.

Now let's turn our attention to how we spend our money. Once we've established biblical priorities concerning giving, saving, debt, and credit, we also need to apply similar principles to spending.

7

Spending

How should we spend our money? It's an important question to ask and answer effectively. During our lifetimes, a large sum of money passes through our hands, as noted in chapter 2. Consider that the average household income in the U.S. is around $50,000. That means that within two decades a million dollars passes through that family!

How we handle our finances says a great deal about our emotional and spiritual maturity. For some people spending money is an addictive behavior similar to other addictive behaviors. (Later in this chapter we will address the issue of compulsive spending.)

But all of us can measure our ability to control our behavior by looking at how we spend money. Self-control is a fruit of the Spirit (Galatians 5:23). The Bible also warns us of the dangers a person who lacks self-control is in (Proverbs 25:28). So let's begin by looking at how we can exercise self-control so we spend less and save more.

How can I spend less money?

One of the ways to make the most of your money in tough times is to look for ways to economize. Over the years, many consumer groups have published lists of various ways to keep from wasting money. Let's look at some of those suggestions.

Don't buy a new car. Cars depreciate fastest during the first few years you own them. To put it simply, "That new car smell will cost you 30 percent." If you go out and purchase the same car used, you will save 30 percent or more. In fact, the cheapest car you will ever have is the one you have right now.

My last two cars have been "program cars." These are cars that a company bought new and then put up for sale after there was 20,000 miles on them. These cars have been such a great buy and have lasted for years and years.

By the way, there are other hidden costs in addition to the cost of a new car. Used cars typically have lower insurance premiums because the car costs less. So you not only save on the upfront purchase but on the insurance premiums.

> ### Don't throw away your money
>
> A new car that sells for $28,000 will lose about $17,000 of value in the first four years you own it. Dave Ramsey says that is like throwing a $100 bill out the window on the way to work every week for four years.[1]

Don't buy brand names at the supermarket and drugstore. Although it's true that some brand-name items are worth the extra money, most are not. In most cases, generic or house-label versions of the brand-name goods are just as good and cost much less. It's worth checking labels and ingredients. You'll find that most of the time the house or generic items are made with the same ingredients and same formulas as the brand-name ones. Many times they're even made by the same companies! Since supermarkets and drugstores don't need to advertise these products, their house-label lines of products and drugs are cheaper. Most consumer-shopping Web sites have lists of generic products that are a good buy, as well as a list of those that aren't worth buying.

Purchase basic clothing. If you have to limit your shopping budget, focus on the basics. Modest clothing that isn't too radical will last you through time. Trying to stay up-to-date with every fashion trend is a quick way to spend more than you should.

Don't eat out so often. A nice dinner out with the family is fine, but eating out regularly really adds up. Consider that restaurants make a gross markup on food of 60 to 70 percent. Then there are taxes and tips of about 15 to 20 percent. Multiply that by a few times a week and then multiply that by 52 weeks. This quickly adds up to lots of money.

When you do go to a restaurant, there are some important principles. Think about sharing a meal. Just because restaurants have enlarged their portions doesn't mean you need to eat everything set before you. Also consider the "doggie bag." Tonight's dinner could also be tomorrow's lunch.

Repair it yourself. Unless you have access to a very inexpensive handyman, you'll probably save lots of money by trying to repair things around your home. You may not be very handy, but fortunately there are Web sites and even home-improvement stores that can give you lots of help and essential tips.

Do your own chores. You may be in the habit of having other people mow your lawn, paint your house, and even wash your car. These are all tasks you probably used to do at one point and can probably do again and save money in the process. It's also a great way to get some more exercise (something nearly all of us need more of these days).

Spend less on food. Two of the quickest ways to spend less on food are to buy in bulk at the grocery store and to clip coupons. There are whole Web sites and books devoted to saving money on food purchases. Others instruct you in how to buy and cook in bulk and freeze prepared food for future use.

Shop for cheaper homeowner's insurance. We already discussed this in the previous chapter, but let me emphasize two important points.

1. Most of us pay our home-insurance premiums the same way we pay the light bill. We don't even think about shopping for a cheaper policy. Even if you keep your existing policy,

you should ask your insurer for discounts you qualify for. For example, if your car insurance and home insurance are with the same company, you might qualify for a discount of 5 percent to 15 percent. You might qualify for a discount if you are a member of certain organizations (for example, AARP, AAA).

2. By making certain improvements to your home, you might qualify for a discount. Homeowners who live in a hurricane zone can install special protection for walls and windows and qualify. Installing smoke detectors or carbon monoxide detectors may also help you qualify.

Consider the cost of canceling your cell-phone contract. Currently cell-phone companies tie you into a two-year contract. Canceling it can cost as much as $200 per phone. Each year consumers spend more than a billion dollars on early termination fees. Reconsider canceling.

If you must cancel the contract, consider contacting one of the companies that help you transfer it to someone else. These companies are like cell-phone matchmakers, who connect people trying to cancel their service with others willing to take it over.

And while we're talking about cell phones, try to find a service that doesn't charge you for every text message. Often you pay 10 cents per message for a technology that's the same as the current phone service voice calls. It should be free to a fixed charge per month. Otherwise you will spend lots of money on text messages.

Take advantage of company benefits. When someone talks about company benefits, we usually think of retirement accounts and health insurance. But there are many other company benefits we often forget to utilize. Many companies offer health savings accounts and flexible-spending accounts. These could significantly save you money on medical expenses.

Some companies have memberships with discount shopping clubs.

They also have group-purchasing discounts (even on such items as car insurance and home insurance). Nearly one-fourth of companies offer employees entertainment discounts (which allow them to purchase tickets to the symphony or the local movie theater for less). Check into these various company discounts. They could save you a lot of money.

American spending
Americans spend more than $7 billion on movies each year, and spend more than $450 billion each Christmas season.[2]

Watch the waste. Waste can hurt your wallet. Think about every time you leave a light on when you leave the room. Don't let water drip or the car idle for long periods of time. If you add up all the money you spend on things you waste, you'll find lots of discretionary income you never knew you had.

What are the symptoms of compulsive spending?

We should be aware that we live in a society that promotes compulsive spending. Each day we're bombarded by advertising slogans and messages. These are designed to get us to buy more than we need. They promise to make us popular and successful. Sometimes they play on our inadequacies and insecurities. Advertising fuels consumer demand, but consumers without a measure of self-control fall into the trap of compulsive spending.

Compulsive spending is actually an addiction that's similar to other addictions (alcoholism, drug abuse, gambling, food disorders). People who continually buy on impulse or "shop till they drop" may be manifesting a form of it.

Why do people engage in compulsive spending? Shopping makes them feel better. Many even say they get a high or a "rush" like you would receive from other addictions.

Now, everyone overspends at one time or another. We see a bargain and can't pass it up. We see a new piece of technology and are convinced we can't live without it. However, there is a fundamental difference between an occasional impulse buy and compulsive spending. Here are a few major symptoms:

1. *Buying what you don't need.* Compulsive shoppers may go on buying binges where they purchase multiple items of the same kind (shoes, clothes, and so on). They may even have clothes in their closet with the price tags still attached.

2. *Addiction to credit cards.* If you feel like you can't live without your credit cards, you may be guilty of compulsive spending. When you use cash for purchases, there are natural limits to your spending. Credit cards let you spend more money than you have.

3. *Busting the budget.* Buying items on credit allows you to spend more than you have. If each month you have more month than you have money, the problem may be compulsive spending.

4. *"Creative financing."* If you're juggling accounts and bills in order to accommodate your spending habits, compulsive spending could be your problem. If you're using one credit card to pay off a different credit card, you have a spending problem. If you can barely make the minimum payment on a credit card, you've exceeded your financial limits.

5. *The feeling of "I can't help myself."* If you feel like you can't control your spending, you may be a compulsive spender. Spending money may feel reckless. Your spending habits may leave you feeling guilty, ashamed, or embarrassed.

6. *Family arguments over finances.* If you're having arguments with others (spouse, parents, and so on) regarding shopping or spending habits, you may be spending compulsively. Sometimes compulsive spending isn't the cause (emotional distress) but the result (compensating for problems). You may be spending to make yourself feel good

about yourself. Buying something new feels good, at least for a short time.

7. *Lying about purchases.* In order to avoid family arguments over finances, you lie about what you bought or how much money you spent on purchases. Sometimes the compulsive shopper isn't lying. He or she may not even remember buying an item because an emotional blackout occurred at the time.

The reasons behind compulsive spending are numerous, and many of them are hinted at in the symptoms listed above. Social scientists have found that one common denominator is *low self-esteem.* Buying things makes people feel better about themselves for a short time. This is the "instant gratification" syndrome that can be a part of addiction.

Another common denominator is *ineffective impulse control.* Compulsive spenders buy on a whim. It's the "I want it now" syndrome that fuels so much consumer spending. Compulsive spenders lack financial self-control and make unplanned purchases. As we mentioned before, self-control is a fruit of the Spirit (Galatians 5:23). Believers should develop self-control by putting on the new self (Colossians 3:1-12) since we have died with Christ and are freed from sin (Romans 6).

Materialism is another reason for compulsive spending. Most consumers have never stopped to make a distinction between needs and wants. Obviously, food, clothing, and shelter are needs (although much of what we spend even in these categories might be considered excessive). We should resist the temptation of materialism. Paul writes to Timothy about those "who want to get rich" who "fall into temptation" and this will "plunge men into ruin and destruction" (1 Timothy 6:9). He therefore warns that "the love of money is a root of all sorts of evil" (verse 10).

Financial ignorance is also a reason for compulsive spending. Most couples do not have a budget and lack basic knowledge about spending, debt, and credit. The obvious solution is to develop a budget and live within it. Another is to learn more about basic financial principles based upon the Bible.

How can I control compulsive spending?

When people have a compulsive behavior, the best solution is to stop the behavior altogether. Unfortunately, most of us have to spend to live. It's the same as with compulsive eating. We have to eat to live. Likewise, we have to spend to live. So stopping spending is difficult unless we give that responsibility completely over to someone else.

People with a compulsive eating disorder have to learn to control their eating and therefore eat sensibly. Likewise, compulsive spenders need to learn how to handle money sensibly and use discipline in their spending habits.

Some of the principles already discussed in the chapter on debt apply here. You may need to cut up your credit cards or give them to someone else to keep so you won't be tempted to use them. You should refrain from taking out any loans. The first lesson when you find yourself down in a hole: *Stop digging.* If you're in debt, taking out a loan will merely fuel more compulsive spending. And you should develop a realistic budget for both income and spending.

When you prove yourself faithful in financial matters, God will bless you with new responsibilities. Jesus said, "If you have not been faithful in the use of unrighteous wealth, who will entrust the true riches to you?" (Luke 16:11). When we handle the small things that God has put under our authority, He will entrust greater things to us.

Since spending money can be like other addictive behaviors, it is also important to address this in our spiritual life. As noted earlier, we should cultivate the fruit of the Spirit, especially self-control (Galatians 5:23). The Bible warns us of the danger a person is in who lacks self-control: "Like a city whose walls are broken down is a man who lacks self-control" (Proverbs 25:28 NIV).

Self-control comes from internal self-discipline. But self-control can also come from external means such as a budget. When you are considering a purchase, it's worth asking if it is in your budget. If it's not in your budget, what will you change in your budget in order to make this purchase?

Self-control also takes wisdom and discernment. An item on sale may seem like a savings, but it still requires that you spend money to purchase it. Spending is not saving. Perhaps you've seen the cartoon of the wife arriving home with lots of shopping bags—she announces to her husband, "Boy, did I save you money!" When you *spend* money you aren't *saving* money. You may be saving money from what you originally budgeted, but you're still spending it.

> **Get to the root**
>
> In some cases, a compulsive spender might want to seek professional counseling. This addiction (like other addictions) may have an underlying issue that a trained, biblical counselor can address. Often addictive behaviors are related and come in clusters. A counselor can help get to the root problem.

Wise shoppers also consider the future costs of an item. When you buy a car, you're dedicating yourself to many other purchases (gas, oil, tires, repairs). These should all be budgeted items as well.

Accountability is another important principle. If spending is a problem, be accountable to someone else.

> Two are better than one because they have a good return for their labor. For if either of them falls, the one will lift up his companion. But woe to the one who falls when there is not another to lift him up (Ecclesiastes 4:9-10).

Again, learn to distinguish between wants and needs. A compulsive eater needs food, but he or she doesn't need 5000 calories a day. Likewise, as mentioned, a compulsive spender needs food, clothing, and shelter, but not all the other things he or she is tempted to buy each day.

If you do have something you want to buy, consider creating a "want-to-buy" sheet. Write it down and wait a week to see if you are still convinced you need it. During that time search out comparative prices for the item and talk to your accountability partner. Only after doing all this should you consider buying it.

～

In these first seven chapters, we've talked about how to apply biblical principles to your personal finances. In the final chapters of this book we're going to look at how to apply the Bible to the broader area of economics.

8

The Bible *and* Economics

Throughout this book we've focused most of our attention on household finances and what could best be called "applied economics." But another important area is the philosophical and biblical foundations for our economic system. In this chapter we'll explore the biblical basis for economics, as well as the basis for the free-market system and economic and moral criticisms that some people have of capitalism.

What does the Bible have to say about economics?

The Bible provides a firm moral foundation for economics, but that's not how economics is taught today. A few centuries ago, there was much greater emphasis given to its moral aspects.

For example, if you look at the *Summa Theologica* of Thomas Aquinas, you find whole sections of his great theological work devoted to economic issues. He asked such questions as "What is a just price?" and "How should we deal with poverty?"

Today, these questions, if they're even discussed at all, are discussed in a class on economic theory. But in Aquinas's time, these were theological questions that were a critical and integral part of educational curricula.

With the Protestant Reformation, we find the same thing. In John Calvin's *Institutes of the Christian Religion*, whole sections are devoted to government and economics. So Christians should not feel that economics is outside the domain of Christian thinking. If anything, we need to recapture this arena and bring a strong biblical message to it.

There's no utopia

Christians should see the fallacy of utopian economic theories, such as Marxism, because they fail to take human sinfulness seriously. Instead of teaching that change in people comes from the inside out, as the gospel does, Marxists believe that people will be changed from the outside in. Change the economic structure, they say, and you will change human beings. This is one of the reasons Marxism was doomed to failure—because it didn't take into account human sinfulness and our need for spiritual redemption.

As we saw earlier, the Bible speaks to economic issues more than any other issue. Whole sections of the book of Proverbs and the prophetic books and many of the parables of Jesus deal with economic matters. They tell us what our attitude should be toward wealth and how a believer should handle his or her finances. The Bible also provides a description of human nature, which helps us evaluate the possible success of an economic system in society.

The Bible teaches that there are two aspects to human nature. First, we're created in the image of God and are thus able to control the economic system. But second, human beings are sinful and thus tend toward greed and exploitation. This points to the need to protect individuals from human sinfulness in the economic system. So Christians have a balanced view of economics, from which they can construct economic theories and analyze existing economic systems.

How does a biblical view of human nature allow us to analyze economics?

When we're looking at either theories of government or theories of economics, an important starting point is our view of human nature. This helps us analyze such theories and predict their outcome in society. Therefore, we must go to the Scriptures to evaluate the very foundation of each economic theory.

First, the Bible says that human beings are created in the image of God. This implies that we have rationality and responsibility. Because we have rationality and volition, we can choose between various competing products and services. Furthermore, we can function within a market system in which people can exercise their power of choice. We are not like the animals, which are governed by instinct. We are governed by rationality and can make meaningful choices within a market system.

We can also assume that private property can exist within this system, because of the biblical concept of dominion. In Genesis 1:28, God says we are to subdue the earth and have dominion over the creation. Certainly one aspect of this is that humans can own property over which they can exercise their dominion.

Since we have both volition and private-property rights, we can then assume that we should have the freedom to exchange these private-property rights in a market where goods and services can be freely exchanged.

The second part of human nature is also important. The Bible describes the fall of the world and the fall of mankind. We are fallen creatures with a sin nature. This sinfulness manifests itself in selfishness, greed, and exploitation. Thus, we need some protection in an economic system from the sinful effects of human interaction.

Since the Bible teaches about the effects of sinful behavior on the world, we should be concerned about any system that might concentrate economic power and thereby unleash the ravages of sinful behavior on a society. Christians, therefore, should reject state-controlled or centrally controlled economies, which would concentrate power in the hands of a few sinful individuals. Instead, we should support an economic system that disperses that power and protects us from greed and exploitation.

Finally, we should also recognize that not only is human nature fallen, but the world is fallen. The world has become a place of decay and scarcity. In a fallen world, we have to be good managers of the limited resources that can be made available in a market economy. God has given us dominion over His creation, and we must be good stewards of the resources at our disposal.

A biblical view of private property

The Bible provides some general principles related to property. First, as mentioned in a previous chapter, the Bible clearly teaches that everything in the world belongs to the Lord. Psalm 24:1 says, "The earth is the LORD's, and all it contains, the world, and those who dwell in it."

At the same time, as we noted, the Bible also teaches that we are given dominion over the creation (Genesis 1:28). We are accountable to God for our stewardship of the resources.

Because God owns it all (Psalm 24:1), no one owns property in perpetuity. But the Bible does grant private-property rights to individuals. One of the Ten Commandments prohibits stealing, thus approving of private-property rights. The book of Exodus establishes the rights of property owners and the liabilities of those who violate those rights. Financial restitution (Exodus 22) must be made to property owners in case of theft or neglect. Physical force is allowed to protect property (Exodus 22:2). Lost animals are to be returned, even when they belong to an enemy (Exodus 23:4). Removing landmarks that protect property is clearly forbidden (Deuteronomy 19:14; 27:17; Job 24:2; Proverbs 22:28; Hosea 5:10).

Because the book of Acts teaches that the early Christians held property in common, some Christians have suggested that the New Testament rejects the idea of private property. But this communal sharing in the New Testament was voluntary. Acts 2:44-47 says,

> All those who had believed were together and had all
> things in common; and they began selling their property

and possessions and were sharing them with all, as anyone might have need. Day by day continuing with one mind in the temple, and breaking bread from house to house, they were taking their meals together with gladness and sincerity of heart, praising God and having favor with all the people. And the Lord was adding to their number day by day those who were being saved.

The early Christians did not reject the idea of private property. Notice that they still retained private-property rights until they voluntarily gave up those rights to help other believers in Jerusalem. This was a specific leading of the Holy Spirit to meet the increasing needs of the growing New Testament church.

The Pilgrims and private property

When the Pilgrims landed at Plymouth, they were originally organized on a communal basis according to their charter. The land was owned in common so that each person's labor contributed to the community. The results were disastrous.

William Bradford saw that their communal system encouraged laziness and inefficiency, so he changed it. In its place he established private-property rights and distributed plots of land among the Pilgrims. This encouraged individual initiative and was very successful. He recorded the Pilgrims' success with private property in his diaries.[1]

We can see that they retained property rights in the actions of Ananias and Sapphira. Their sin was not that they retained control of some of their property but that they lied about it. Peter asks them in Acts 5:4, "While it remained unsold, did it not remain your own? And after it was sold, was it not under your control? Why is it that you have conceived this deed in your heart? You have not lied to men but to God."

Also notice that Paul called for voluntary charity toward believers in Jerusalem when he called New Testament believers to give to the needs of those within the church. Second Corinthians 8:13-15 says,

> This is not for the ease of others and for your affliction, but by way of equality—at this present time your abundance being a supply for their need, so that their abundance also may become a supply for your need, that there may be equality; as it is written, "He who gathered much did not have too much, and he who gathered little had no lack."

A biblical view of work

What is the place of work in economic activity? We should begin by clearing up a major misconception. Many Christians think that we work because of the fall (Genesis 3). Actually that's not true. Work is not a product of the fall but is actually part of the creation order (Genesis 2:15-17). However, it's true that work was deformed by the fall so that there is now toil and drudgery.

However, *God created us to work the land and be productive.* Through work we are given the opportunity to design and create. Because of Christ's redemptive work on our behalf, all of us can be involved in meaningful work that is good and reflects His redemptive purpose.

Second, *we're created in God's image (Genesis 1:27), so we can find work rewarding and empowering.* We're given the privilege by God of enjoying the earth and deriving profit and benefit from what it might produce (Genesis 9:1-3). At the same time, we should also be held accountable for the work we do or fail to do. When Paul wrote to the Thessalonians, he devoted a portion of his epistles to the importance of work for the Christian. In 1 Thessalonians 4:11-12 he said "Make it your ambition to lead a quiet life and attend to your own business and work with your hands, just as we commanded you, so that you will behave properly toward outsiders and not be in any need." He also warns in 2 Thessalonians 3:10 that "if anyone is not willing to work, then he is not to eat, either."

Third, *there is also a satisfaction in work*. It not only satisfies a basic human need but it also is a privilege provided by the hand of God. Ecclesiastes 2:24 says, "There is nothing better for a man than to eat and drink and tell himself that his labor is good. This also I have seen that it is from the hand of God."

The Proverbs talk about the importance and benefits of work. Proverbs 12:11 says, "He who tills his land will have plenty of bread, but he who pursues worthless things lacks sense." Proverbs 13:4 says: "The soul of the sluggard craves and gets nothing, but the soul of the diligent is made fat." And 14:23 says: "In all labor there is profit, but mere talk leads only to poverty."

Fourth, *we are to work unto the Lord*. Paul admonishes believers to "work heartily as for the Lord rather than for men" (Colossians 3:23). Paul also says in 1 Corinthians 1:26-31,

> Consider your calling, brethren, that there were not many wise according to the flesh, not many mighty, not many noble; but God has chosen the foolish things of the world to shame the wise, and God has chosen the weak things of the world to shame the things which are strong, and the base things of the world and the despised God has chosen, the things that are not, so that He may nullify the things that are, so that no man may boast before God. But by His doing you are in Christ Jesus, who became to us wisdom from God, and righteousness and sanctification, and redemption, so that, just as it is written, "Let him who boasts, boast in the Lord."

We also learn from Scripture that without God's involvement in our work, human labor is futile. Psalm 127:1 says, "Unless the LORD builds the house, they labor in vain who build it." God's blessings come to us through our labors.

Finally, *with work there should also be rest*. The law of the Sabbath (Exodus 20:8-11) and the other Old Testament provisions for feasts and rest demonstrate the importance of rest. In the New Testament also we see that Jesus set a pattern for rest (Mark 6:45-47; Luke 6:12) in His ministry. Believers are to work for the Lord and His kingdom, but they must also avoid being workaholics and take time to rest.

We should also mention the opposite of work. The Bible warns us of the consequences of idleness. Proverbs 24:30-34 says,

> I passed by the field of the sluggard and by the vineyard of the man lacking sense, and behold, it was completely overgrown with thistles; its surface was covered with nettles and its stone wall was broken down. When I saw, I reflected upon it; I looked, and received instruction. "A little sleep, a little slumber, a little folding of the hands to rest," then your poverty will come as a robber and your want like an armed man.

What is the role of government in the economic arena?

The Bible gives some clear principles concerning government. First, Christians are commanded to obey government (Romans 13:1) and submit to civil authority (1 Peter 2:13-17). We are called to render service and obedience to the government (Matthew 22:21). However, we are not to render total submission. There may be a time when Christians may be called to disobey government leaders who have set themselves in opposition to divine law (Romans 13:1-5; John 19:11). We are to obey civil authorities (Roman 13:5) in order to avoid anarchy and chaos, but there may be times when we may be forced to obey God rather than men (Acts 5:29).

Second, we understand that because of the fall (Genesis 3), all have a sin nature (Romans 3:23). Government must therefore administer justice in the political and economic realm. It must also protect us against aggression as well as provide for public works (1 Kings 10:9).

The reality of the sin nature dictates that, as noted earlier, we not allow a political concentration of power. Governmental power should be limited with appropriate checks and balances. Government also should not be used in a coercive way to attempt to change individuals. We should not accept the idea that the state can transform people from the outside. Only the gospel can change people from the inside so they become new creatures (2 Corinthians 5:17).

Consider these four functions of government in the economic realm. Government must ensure justice in the following ways:[2]

- "Weights and scales are to be honest, a full measure (shaken down) is to be given (Leviticus 19:35-36; Deuteronomy 25:15; Proverbs 20:23; Luke 6:38), and currency is not to be debased by inflationary monetary policy or other means (for example, mixing lead with silver)."

- Procedural justice requires that contracts and commitments be honored (Leviticus 19:13).

- Government must also ensure justice when people are cheated or swindled. In these cases, the cost of restoration should be borne by the guilty or negligent party (Exodus 21:33-36; 22:5-8,10-15). Government should also deal with those who give a false accusation (Deuteronomy 19:16-19).

- Government should also prevent economic discrimination. This would apply to those of different economic class (James 2:1-4) as well as to those of different sex, race, and religious background (Galatians 3:26-29). Government can exert a great influence on the economy and therefore should use its regulatory power to protect against discrimination.

That being said, the primary function of government is to set the rules and provide a means of redress. The free market should be allowed to function with government providing the necessary economic boundaries and protections. Once this is done, in the free-enterprise system individuals are free to use their economic choices in a free market.

What is the foundation of the free-enterprise system?

The philosophical foundation for capitalism can be found in *The Wealth of Nations*, written by Adam Smith in 1776. He argued that the economic system of mercantilism that held sway at that time in Great Britain was not the best. Instead, he argued that the wealth of nations could be increased by allowing the individual to seek his own self-interest and by removing government control over the economy.

His theory rested on three major premises. First, his system was based upon the observation that *people are motivated by self-interest*. He said, "It is not from the benevolence of the butcher, the brewer, or the baker that we expect our dinner, but from their regard to their own interest." Smith went on to say that "neither intends to promote the public interest," yet each is "led by an invisible hand to promote an end that was not part of [his] intention."[3]

A second premise of Smith was *the acceptance of private property*. Property was not to be held in common but owned and freely traded in a market system. Profits generated from the use and exchange of private property rights provided incentive and became the mechanism that drove the capitalist system.

From a Christian perspective we can see that the basis of private property rests in our being created in God's image. We can make choices over property that we can exchange in a market system. The need for private property grows out of our sinfulness. Our sinful nature produces laziness, neglect, and slothfulness. Economic justice can best be achieved if each person is accountable for his own productivity.

A third premise of Smith's theory was *the minimization of the role of government*. Borrowing a phrase from the French physiocrats, he called this principle *laissez-faire*. Smith argued that we should decrease the role of government and increase the role of a free market.

Historically, capitalism has had a number of advantages. It has liberated economic potential. It has also provided the foundation for a great deal of political and economic freedom. When government isn't controlling markets, then there is freedom to be involved in a whole array of entrepreneurial activities.

Capitalism has also led to a great deal of political freedom because once you limit the role of government in economics, you limit the scope of government in other areas. It's no accident that most of the countries with the greatest political freedom usually have a great deal of economic freedom.

What are some of the economic criticisms of capitalism?

The first economic criticism of capitalism is that *it leads to monopolies*. These develop for two reasons: too little government and too much government. Monopolies have occurred in the past because government hasn't been willing to exercise its God-given authority. In the United States, the government finally stepped in and broke up the big trusts that were not allowing the free-enterprise system to function correctly.

But in recent decades, the reason for monopolies has often been too much government. Many of the largest monopolies today are government sanctioned or sponsored monopolies that prevent true competition from taking place. The solution is for government to allow a freer market, where competition can take place.

Let me add that many people often call markets with limited competition monopolies when the term is not appropriate. For example, the major car companies may seem like a monopoly or oligopoly until you realize that in the market of consumer durables the true market is the entire Western world.

The second criticism of capitalism is that *it leads to pollution*. In a capitalistic system, pollutants are considered externalities. In controlling them, the producer will incur costs that are external to the firm so often there is no incentive to clean up the pollution. Instead, it is dumped into areas held in common, such as the air or water.

The solution in this case is governmental regulation. But this need not be a justification for building a massive bureaucracy. We need to find creative ways to direct self-interest so people work toward the common good.

Sometimes when speaking on the topic of government and the environment, I use a thought experiment. Most communities use the water supply from a river and dump treated waste back into the water to flow downstream. Often there is a tendency to cut corners and leave the waste-treatment problem for those downstream. But imagine if you required that the water-intake pipe be downstream and the waste pipe be upstream. If you did require this (and this is only a thought experiment) you would instantly guarantee that you'd have less of a problem with water pollution. Why? It's now in the self-interest of the community to clean the wastewater being pumped back into the river. So while there is a need for governmental action, much less might be needed if we thought of creative ways to constrain self-interest and make it work for the common good.

> **Use careful judgment**
>
> Christians shouldn't endorse every aspect of capitalism. For example, many proponents of capitalism hold a view known as *utilitarianism*, which is opposed to the notion of biblical absolutes. Certainly we must reject this philosophy as well as some of the abuses of capitalism.

We can acknowledge that although there are some valid economic criticisms of capitalism, these can be addressed by limited governmental control. And when capitalism is wisely controlled, it generates significant economic prosperity and economic freedom for its citizens.

What are some of the moral criticisms of capitalism?

One of the moral arguments against capitalism involves the issue of greed. And this is why many Christians feel ambivalent toward the free-enterprise system. After all, some critics of capitalism contend that this economic system makes people greedy.

To answer this question we need to resolve the following issue:

Does capitalism make people greedy, or do we already have greedy people, who then use the economic freedom of the capitalistic system to achieve their ends? In light of the biblical description of human nature, the latter seems more likely.

Because people are sinful and selfish, some are going to use the capitalist system to feed their greed. But that's not so much a criticism of capitalism as it's a recognition of the human condition. The goal of capitalism isn't to change people, but to protect us from human sinfulness.

Capitalism is a system in which bad people can do the least harm, and good people have the freedom to do good works. It works well if you have completely moral individuals. But it also functions adequately when you have selfish and greedy people.

Important to this discussion is the understanding that there's a difference between *self-interest* and *selfishness*. All people have self-interest, and that can operate in ways that are not selfish. For example, it's in my self-interest to get a job and earn an income so I can support my family. I can do that in ways that aren't selfish. Adam Smith recognized that every one of us has self-interest, and rather than trying to change that, he made self-interest the motor of the capitalist system.

By contrast, other economic systems, like socialism, ignore the biblical definitions of human nature. Thus, they allow economic power to be centralized, and they concentrate power in the hands of a few greedy people. Those who complain of the influence major corporations have on our lives should consider the socialist alternative of how a few governmental bureaucrats would control every aspect of their lives.

Greed certainly occurs in the capitalist system. But it doesn't surface just in this economic system. It's part of our sinfulness. Capitalism may have its flaws as an economic system, but it can be controlled to give us a great deal of economic prosperity and economic freedom.

9

Economic Questions

Although we've discussed many different economic issues in the previous chapters, there remain some important questions that deserve an answer. Subjects like the cost of government, taxes, the Federal Reserve, and inflation are all in the news. It's important to understand these issues and factors in order to be a wise steward of the financial resources you have.

The real cost of government

Most people don't even realize how much they pay in taxes. And they're certainly unaware of how much government costs them when both its direct costs and indirect costs (through such things as government regulations) are calculated.

To help us understand, various groups have run the numbers and designated certain days on the calendar to illustrate the true cost of government. One such measure of government is "Tax Freedom Day," designated each year by the Tax Foundation.[1] For the last two decades Tax Freedom Day has usually fallen during the month of April (although two years it was in early May). This is the day of the year by which Americans have earned enough income to pay their taxes. Put another way, you are working for the government for the first four months of the year.

Tax Freedom Day is calculated by taking the official government figure for total tax collections and dividing it by the nation's total income. That percentage (most recently 30.8 percent) is used to calculate the number of days in the year we collectively must work before we enjoy freedom from taxes.

It is worth noting that Tax Freedom Day varies from state to state. Residents of Alaska kick it off a week before any other state. And the residents of the state of California must wait until the very end of April.

It is also worth noting that Tax Freedom Day used to be very early in the year. For example, in 1900 it was January 22. By 1920 it was February 13, and by 1940 it was March 7.

Another important measure is "Cost of Government Day," which is calculated by Americans for Tax Reform.[2] This measure looks at both taxes and regulations. Cost of Government Day is currently in the middle of July. On that day, the average American has finally paid his or her share of the financial burden imposed by both spending and regulation on the federal, state, and local levels.

Think about that for a moment. It takes a little more than half of the year to finally get government off your back so you can begin to earn a living for you and your family. And what's even more disturbing is that the cost of government in terms of spending and regulation is increasing faster than national income. That suggests that Cost of Government Day will come later and later each year.

We all can agree that government is necessary and does some good. But when taxpayers begin to realize that they spend half their life working for government, often they stop and wonder how it happened. The answer is that government has grown incrementally. Each generation allows government to grow, and the

---

The tax burden

The rich in America pay a large share of the taxes. The top 1 percent paid 40 percent of all income taxes in 2006. The top 10 percent paid 71 percent, and the top 50 percent paid 97 percent of all income taxes.

next generation takes that growth for granted and allows more to take place. Each year government controls more of our lives.

The cost of regulation by government is often hidden, but some organizations have attempted to put it in monetary terms. The Competitive Enterprise Institute has estimated that the yearly cost of federal regulation has now grown to over one trillion dollars.[3] Put another way, federal government regulations cost nearly 10 percent of what the U.S. economy produces each year.

While we would all acknowledge that we need *some* government regulations, you have to begin to question whether they are all necessary and effective, especially when they're costing us one trillion dollars each year. To put this in perspective, government spending in the last few years has been over two trillion dollars. So the hidden tax of regulation now approaches half the level of federal spending itself. Put another way, regulations cost about as much as individual income tax collections.

The Competitive Enterprise Institute has another document called "Ten Thousand Commandments: An Annual Snapshot of the Federal Regulatory State."[4] You have to love that turn of phrase. Today Americans are burdened by government's 10,000 commandments. In essence, government has issued 10,000 commandments to try to enforce the Ten Commandments.

Do taxes affect where people live?

There's an old adage: "High taxes don't redistribute income, they redistribute people." The point is that people vote with their feet. And there's abundant evidence that Americans have been moving from high-tax states to low-tax states.

A 2007 survey uncovered some interesting patterns of movement in America.[5] An average of 20,000 Americans relocate across state lines each day, adding up to about eight million Americans each year. The general pattern is for people to move from the Northeast and Midwest to the South and West. But the details are even more interesting than these general trends.

The survey found that the most reliable indicator of movement was income tax. People tend to move from states with high income-tax rates to states with little or no income tax. Families are leaving Michigan, New York, New Jersey, Ohio, Pennsylvania, and Illinois. Contrast that with the 8 states among the lower 48 that have no income tax (Florida, Nevada, New Hampshire, South Dakota, Tennessee, Texas, Washington, and Wyoming). Every one of these states gained in net domestic migrants. And each one except Florida (which has sky-high property taxes) "ranked in the top 12 of destination states."

In order to see the phenomenon close-up, compare North Dakota to South Dakota. Both states are essentially the same in terms of geography and climate. But they couldn't be more different in terms of migration. North Dakota lost a greater percentage of citizens than any other state except Michigan. South Dakota ranked in the top 12 states as a target of net domestic migration. People are moving out of North Dakota, but they're moving to South Dakota in droves. North Dakota has an income tax. South Dakota does not.

For many years now, demographers have noted the flight of upper-income, educated families from California. California was the only Pacific Coast state to lose population by interstate migration in 2007. One of the major reasons is that California has the highest state income tax in the nation. More than one and a half million Californians have left the state in the last ten years.

Where are many of these people going? They are moving to neighboring Nevada, which has no income tax. "High-income Californians can buy a house in Las Vegas for the amount they save in three or four years by not paying California income taxes."

It's also worth noting that one of the few Northeastern states that gained interstate migrants was New Hampshire. Why? New Hampshire is the only state in New England without an income tax.

Is America going broke?

Let me ask a provocative question. Is America going broke? Many have asked the question, but when an economist asks it, it creates quite a stir. In 2006, Laurence Kotlikoff asked, "Is the United States bankrupt?"[6] He concluded that countries can go broke and that the United States is going broke due to future obligations to Social Security and Medicare. At the time, his commentary generated lots of discussion and controversy.

Two years later Kotlikoff, writing for *Forbes* magazine, asked the question in a slightly different way: "Is the U.S. going broke?"[7] He pointed out that the federal government's takeover of Fannie Mae and Freddie Mac in 2008 represented a major financial challenge. These two institutions issued about half of the mortgages in America. Part of the federal bailout of these institutions put the government on the hook for $5 trillion (if you consider the corporate debt that is owed and the mortgage debt that is guaranteed).

But $5 trillion is effectively pocket change when you consider the real liabilities that are facing our government. Kotlikoff estimated in his article that the real liabilities were on the order of $70 trillion. (As we will see in a moment, some estimate our unfunded liabilities at around $100 trillion.)

> **U.S. debt and GDP**
>
> The total U.S. debt as a percentage of GDP changed dramatically starting in the 1980s. From the 1950s to the 1980s, the debt as a percentage was around 200 percent. By the 1990s it was 300 percent, and it has now exceeded 350 percent.

The $70 trillion figure actually represents the fiscal difference between the government's projected spending obligations and all its projected tax receipts. Kotlikoff notes,

> This fiscal gap takes into account Uncle Sam's need to service
> official debt-outstanding U.S. government bonds. But it also
> recognizes all our government's unofficial debts, including

its obligation to the soon-to-be-retired baby boomers to pay
their Social Security and Medicare benefits.[8]

Let's put the figure $70 trillion in perspective. That amount is
larger than the entire capital stock of the United States (all land,
buildings, roads, homes, automobiles, factories, bank accounts, stock
certificates, and consumer durables).[9]

Of the three unfunded liabilities Medicare is currently the one
of greatest concern. While the Social Security shortfall is a problem,
it pales in comparison to the short-
fall for Medicare.

Medicare is a pay-as-you-go
program. It includes three parts.
Medicare Part A covers hospital
stays, Medicare B covers doctor
visits, and Medicare D was recently
added as a drug benefit. Although
some members of Congress warned
about future problems with the
system, most politicians have simply
ignored the potential for a massive shortfall.

> **Government
> debt per capita**
>
> Each day the federal govern-
> ment racks up almost $2 billion
> of debt. Looking at the total debt,
> in simple terms, each citizen now
> "owes" the government $32,000.
> By the year 2010, that figure will
> be $38,000.

How big is the financial shortfall? Let me quote from a speech
given by Richard Fisher, the president and chief executive officer of
the Federal Reserve Bank of Dallas. He says,

> The infinite-horizon present discounted value of the
> unfunded liability for Medicare A is $34.4 trillion. The
> unfunded liability of Medicare B is an additional $34 tril-
> lion. The shortfall for Medicare D adds another $17.2 trillion.
> The total? If you wanted to cover the unfunded liability of
> all three programs today, you would be stuck with an $85.6
> trillion bill. That is more than six times as large as the bill
> for Social Security. It is more than six times the annual
> output of the entire U.S. economy.[10]

There are a number of factors that contribute to this enormous problem:

1. There are the same demographic realities that are affecting Social Security. From 1946 to 1964 we had a baby boom followed by a baby bust. Never has such a large cohort been dependent on such a small cohort to fund their entitlement programs.

2. There is longevity. People are living longer lives than ever before.

3. The cost of medical treatment and technology is increasing. We have better drugs and more sophisticated machines, but these all cost money.

4. We have a new entitlement (the prescription drug program), an unfunded liability one-third greater than all of Social Security.

Richard Fisher says that if you add together the unfunded liabilities from Medicare and Social Security, you come up with a figure that is nearly $100 trillion. "Traditional Medicare composes about 69 percent, the new drug benefit roughly 17 percent and Social Security the remaining 14 percent."[11]

What does this mean to each of us? We currently have a population of over 300 million. If we divide the unfunded liability by the number of people in America, the per-person payment comes to $330,000. Put another way, for a family of four this would be a bill of $1.3 million. That's over 25 times the average household's income.

The Federal Reserve and international money policy

In order to understand what will happen when these unfunded liabilities come due, we need to discuss the Federal Reserve. How did we get to the point where the Federal Reserve controls so much of our lives? Why does it seem that the Federal Reserve always has to bail out the government?

To answer these questions, we need to go back to 1913, when the Federal Reserve was created with the passage of the Federal Reserve Act. A group of bankers (often referred to as the "Monopoly Men") traveled on a sealed train to Jekyll Island, Georgia, using code names to put together a plan to form a central bank. They weren't successful at first, but then were able to get the bill passed during the Christmas season, which President Woodrow Wilson signed. This put enormous power in the hands of these bankers and the chairman of the Federal Reserve.

The best way to understand the power of the Federal Reserve is to understand its power to print money. Back in 1933, Treasury Secretary William Wooden talked about this: "The Reserve Act lets us print all we'll need. And it won't frighten people. It won't look like stage money. It'll be money that looks like money."[12]

Some economists have questioned whether we need a Federal Reserve. After all, the United States didn't have a central bank from 1836 (when President Andrew Jackson closed the Second Bank of the United States) to 1913. The justification for the Federal Reserve Act of 1913 was to prevent bank failure and maintain price stability. If that is the case, then the Federal Reserve has been a failure, according to economist Walter Williams. Maximum bank failures in one year before 1913 were 496 and afterward were 4400. Price stability was better before 1913 than afterward. In the century before the Federal Reserve Act, wholesale prices fell by 6 percent. In the century after, they rose by 1300 percent.[13]

Another key date in economic history is 1944. While World War II was still raging, more than 700 delegates from the Allied nations met at Bretton Woods, New Hampshire, to plan the future. This conference produced the International Monetary Fund and the World Bank.

One of the conference's most important acts was to adopt a monetary policy that maintained the exchange rate of its currency within a fixed value in terms of gold. In a sense, they decided that the currencies of the world would "float" against the U.S. dollar. The dollars were redeemable in gold at the last official price at the U.S. Treasury or Federal Reserve. That price is $42.22 per ounce.

Now fast forward to the late 1960s. A problem developed. The U.S. was involved in the Vietnam War at the same time that President Lyndon Johnson was getting the Great Society programs through Congress. Government was spending too much on both defense and domestic programs. Since the war was unpopular, it wasn't possible to raise taxes, and more borrowing wasn't an option. So the Federal Reserve started printing money to monetize the debt.

The increase in the number of dollars in circulation (the money supply) diluted the value of everyone's paper assets. But printing money did something else. It resulted in a run on the U.S. government's gold supply. Remember that the Bretton Woods agreement said that dollars were redeemable in gold at the price of $42.44 per ounce. But the market price of gold was moving toward $65 per ounce. Banks and governments started dumping dollars (Federal Reserve Notes) at the Federal Reserve at $42.22 for each ounce and then selling the gold for $65 per ounce. It looked like the U.S. Central Bank was about to lose all of its gold.

President Richard Nixon really had only two choices. He could raise the official price of gold to the level of the market price of $65 per ounce. That would devalue the dollar by 50 percent. That wasn't really an option. It would have been political suicide to devalue the dollar that much that fast.

His only other option was to repudiate the Bretton Woods agreement and close the "gold window." That's what he did in 1971, and all the currencies of the world have been sinking ever since. Now it's even easier for the Federal Reserve to print money and monetize the U.S. debt.

Is inflation on the horizon?

In light of what we have discussed concerning the federal debt and the unfunded liabilities, it's relatively easy to predict what will happen in the future. Government does not have $70 trillion dollars (much less $100 trillion dollars) in a reserve to fund these entitlement programs. Government has no money of its own. It obtains it in one of three ways. It must either tax it, borrow it, or print it.

If government raises taxes, it expands its size and scope but it also negatively affects economic growth. Politicians can raise taxes somewhat, but they can't raise them enough to cover our debts and liabilities.

If government borrows money, it competes with the private sector for available capital. But since Americans aren't saving, there isn't that much money to borrow domestically. And there's a limit to how much the U.S. can borrow from other countries.

Sooner or later the government (through the Federal Reserve) will start to print the money. As we look back over the last few decades, we can see that our economic problems have been currency-based. And when you print too much money, you have inflation. Investors will be paid back in devalued dollars. Citizens receiving entitlement payments will be paid in devalued dollars. This will be the result of *fiat money* (money not backed by a physical commodity).

> ### Government borrowing
>
> Each year the United States government borrows nearly two-thirds of all the money that is borrowed in the world. This is ten times as much as the next borrower.

In previous centuries, kings and citizens engaged in coin-clipping (shaving the edges off coins). This was a form of inflation, but at least it was visible. Today, paying back investors and citizens with devalued dollars is less visible and more insidious.

In what many regard as one of the most important economic books of the twentieth century, British economist John Maynard

Keynes noted how inflation affects a nation and its citizens. He said: "By a continuing process of inflation, governments can confiscate, secretly and unobserved, an important part of the wealth of their citizens."[14]

He also adds that when we debase the currency, it can have a devastating effect, even though most people will not observe its impact.

> There is no subtler, no surer means of overturning the existing basis of society than to debauch the currency. The process engages all the hidden forces of economic law that come down on the side of destruction, and does so in a manner that not one man in a million is able to diagnose.[15]

What is the impact of inflation? The impact is felt in higher prices. In fact, the classical definition of inflation is "a rise in the general level of prices of goods and services in an economy over a period of time."

What will be the impact on you and your family? You can calculate that by using the mathematical "rule of 72." Take the current inflation rate and divide it into the number 72, and that will give you the number of years it will take for prices to double at that rate of inflation.

If inflation is on the horizon and the dollar continues to decline in value, a wise investor will consider owning assets that are a hedge against inflation and the devaluation of the dollar. That's why we talked about gold (and silver) in the chapter on investing. These metals will most likely maintain value as the value of the dollar declines.

Also consider what would happen if just a small percentage of investors began to purchase gold. One analyst estimated that just 1 percent of our core financial markets (worth at that time about $440 billion) would be equivalent of 13 percent of all the gold accumulated throughout human history.[16] And that 1 percent is four times the value of all the gold held by the U.S. government at Fort Knox.

Imagine where the price of gold would be if investors did put part of their assets in gold. Any gold that you own would be worth even more than it is worth right now.

While it's reasonable to assume the price of gold will rise in the future, it's also reasonable to assume that the price of silver will rise as well, perhaps even faster. Demand for silver has been substantially higher than what mining companies have been able to produce. And it is also worth noting that although the government does own gold, it doesn't own silver. So it must go out on the open market to purchase silver to mint the silver coins it produces each year. That implies that the price of silver will also increase.

The key point is this: You don't have to be a prophet to see that our government's federal debt and unfunded liabilities are going to have an impact on your finances and investments. A wise investor will see these trends and make wise financial decisions.

Thriftville vs. Squanderville

Finally, let's look at the issue of trade and the global economy. A wise investor will also consider the impact of our trade deficit and the impact of the global economy on America's businesses and industry.

Warren Buffett tells the story of two side-by-side islands of equal size: Thriftville and Squanderville.[17] On these islands, land is a capital asset. At first, the people on both islands are at a subsistence level and work eight hours a day to meet their needs. But the Thrifts realize that if they work harder and longer, they can produce a surplus of goods they can trade with the Squanders. So the Thrifts decide to do some serious saving and investing and begin to work 16 hours a day. They begin exporting to Squanderville.

The people of Squanderville like the idea of working less. They can begin to live their lives free from toil. So they willingly trade for these goods with "Squanderbonds" that are denominated in "Squanderbucks."

Over time, the citizens of Thriftville accumulate lots of Squanderbonds. Some of the pundits in Squanderville see trouble. They foresee that the Squanders will now have to put in double time to eat and pay off their debt.

At about the same time, the citizens of Thriftville begin to get nervous and wonder if the Squanders will make good on their Squanderbonds (which are essentially IOUs). So the Thrifts start selling their Squanderbonds for Squanderbucks. Then they use the Squanderbucks to buy Squanderville land. Eventually the Thrifts own all of Squanderville.

Now the citizens of Squanderville must pay rent to live on the land, which is owned by the Thrifts. The Squanders feel like they have been colonized by purchase rather than conquest. And they also face a horrible set of circumstances. They now must not only work eight hours in order to eat, but they must work additional hours to service the debt and pay the Thrifts rent on the land they sold to them.

Although this story is fiction, it is a metaphor for the unfortunate current economic circumstances in the United States. As a nation, we've had significant trade deficits and have been able to purchase resources and manufactured goods on credit. But the developing nations are also now able to purchase these goods, and Americans are beginning to be priced out of the market. We've also been a nation that has been more interested in consuming goods than producing them. And we've been more willing to borrow and less willing to save. This also will have an impact as we interact with the global economy.

The global economy

Many books have been written about globalization and the global economy, but one of the most significant is the book by Thomas Friedman entitled *The World Is Flat: A Brief History of the Twenty-First Century*. His contention is that the global playing field has been leveled or flattened by new technologies. He talks about three eras of globalization.

The first era of globalization (he calls it "Globalization 1.0") lasted from when Columbus set sail until around 1800. "It shrank the world from a size large to a size medium. Globalization 1.0 was about countries and muscles."[18] The key change agent in this era was how much muscle your country had (horsepower, wind power, and so on). Driven by such factors as imperialism and even religion, countries broke down walls and began the process of global integration.

The second era (Friedman calls it "Globalization 2.0") lasted from 1800 to 2000, with interruptions during the Great Depression and World Wars I and II. "This era shrank the world from size medium to a size small. In Globalization 2.0, the key agent of change, the dynamic force driving global integration, was multinational companies."[19] At first these were Dutch and English joint-stock companies, and later it was the growth of a global economy due to computers, satellites, and even the Internet.

The dynamic force in Globalization 1.0 was *countries*, while the dynamic force in Globalization 2.0 was *companies*. Friedman contends that Globalization 3.0 will be different because it provides "the newfound power for individuals to collaborate and compete globally."[20]

"Global flatteners"

Friedman also argues that the global playing field has been flattened by new realities. The first flattener, *the fall of the Berlin Wall,* occurred on November 9, 1989, and it

> unleashed forces that ultimately liberated all the captive peoples of the Soviet Empire. But it actually did so much more. It tipped the balance of power across the world toward those advocating democratic, consensual, free-market-oriented governance, and away from those advocating authoritarian rule with centrally planned economies.[21]

The economic change was even more important. The fall of the

Berlin Wall encouraged the free movement of ideas, goods, and services. "When an economic or technological standard emerged and proved itself on the world stage, it was much more quickly adopted after the wall was out of the way."[22]

A second flattener was *Netscape*. This new software (and other Web browsers that were developed later) played a huge role in flattening the world by making the Internet truly interoperable. Until then, there were disconnected islands of information.

We used to go to the post office to send mail—now most of us send digitized mail, known as e-mail, over the Internet. We used to go to bookstores to browse and buy books—now we browse digitally. We used to buy a CD to listen to music—now many of us obtain our digitized music off the Internet and download it to an MP3 player.

Another flattener is *outsourcing*. In many ways, this was made possible when American companies laid fiber-optic cable to India. Ultimately, India became the beneficiary.

India has become very good at producing brainpower, especially in the sciences, engineering, and medicine. There are a limited number of Indian institutions of higher learning within a population of one billion people. The resulting competition produces a phenomenal knowledge meritocracy. Until India was connected to the Internet, many of the graduates would come to America. Fiber-optic cable became the ocean crosser. You no longer need to leave India to be a professional because you can plug into the world from India.

Offshoring is another flattener. Offshoring is when a company takes one of its factories that is operating in Canton, Ohio, and moves the whole factory to Canton, China.

When China joined the World Trade Organization, Beijing and the rest of the world were taken to a new level of offshoring. Companies began to shift production offshore and integrate their products and services into their global supply chains.

The more attractive China makes itself to offshoring, the more attractive other developed and developing countries have to make themselves. This has created a process of competitive flattening and a scramble to give companies the best tax breaks and subsidies.

How has this affected the United States?

> According to the U.S. Department of Commerce, nearly 90 percent of the output from U.S.-owned offshore factories is sold to foreign consumers. But this actually stimulates American exports. There is a variety of studies indicating that every dollar a company invests overseas in an offshore factory yields additional exports for its home country, because roughly one-third of global trade today is within multinational companies.[23]

Another flattener is *supply-chaining.* "No company has been more efficient at improving its supply chain (and thereby flattening the world) than Wal-Mart; and no company epitomizes the tension the supply chains evoke between the consumer in us and the worker in us than Wal-Mart."[24]

Thomas Friedman calls Wal-Mart "the China of companies" because it can use its leverage to grind down any supplier to the last halfpenny. And speaking of China, if Wal-Mart were an individual economy, it would rank as China's eighth-biggest trading partner, ahead of Russia, Australia, and Canada.

Globalization vs. globalism

Although the terms are sometimes used interchangeably, I want to draw some important distinctions between *globalization* and *globalism. Globalization* is used to describe the changes taking place in society and the world due to economic and technological forces. Essentially, we have a global economy and live in the global village.

Globalism is the attempt to draw us together into a new world order with one world government and one world economy. Sometimes this even involves a desire to develop one world religion. I believe we should be concerned about political attempts to form a new world order.

And another flattener is *"in-forming."* A good example of that is Google, which has been the ultimate equalizer. Whether you are a university professor with a high-speed Internet connection or a poor kid in Asia with access to an Internet café, you have the same basic access to research information. Google puts an enormous amount of information at our fingertips. Essentially, all of the information on the Internet is available to anyone, anywhere, at anytime.

How should we respond to globalization?

Anyone looking at this partial list of the flatteners that Thomas Friedman describes can see that globalization has been a mixed bag. For decades previous, futurists had long talked about globalization and a global village. Now many of these forces have made that a reality, and we can see the impact.

We should first recognize that globalization is already taking place. Some of the impact is quite positive, although much of it has been negative. Americans can see the loss of jobs through outsourcing. Some believe that globalization will benefit the rich and transnational companies at the expense of the poor. Some believe it will diminish the role of nations as opposed to world government.

So how should we respond to this continuing trend? First, we should prepare our children and grandchildren for global competition. Thomas Friedman says that when he was growing up his parents would tell him, "Finish your dinner. People in China and India are starving." Today he tells his daughters, "Girls, finish your homework—people in China and India are starving for your jobs."[25]

Another implication is the growing influence of the two countries with the largest populations: China and India. Major companies are looking to these countries for research and development. The twentieth century was called "the American Century." It is likely that the twenty-first century will be "the Asian Century."

China and India represent one-third of the world's population. They will no doubt transform the entire global economy and political landscape. Students of biblical prophecy wonder if these two countries represent the "kings from the east" (Revelation 16:12). In the past, most of the focus was on China. Perhaps the kings (plural) represent both China and India.

Finally, we should take advantage of some of the aspects of globalization. This flattened world has opened up ministry through the Internet and subsequent travel to these countries. My own ministry has now become a global ministry. In the past, those of us in ministry might receive an occasional letter from a foreign country. Today we interact daily with people from countries around the world. These online contacts open up additional opportunities for speaking and ministry overseas.

~

The economic questions we've discussed in this chapter remind us that we're living in a world that's changing. We need to understand the changes that are taking place in the political and economic realms and therefore in the global economy. However, even though the world is changing around us, we also need to understand that the biblical principles set forth in the previous chapters on giving, debt, saving, and spending still apply today.

To be successful and faithful to the Bible we must do more than just read about these principles—we must apply them as well. We shouldn't merely be hearers, but we must also be doers of the Word of God (see James 1:22). My prayer is that you will not only learn these principles but apply them to your life.

A Final Word

Hopefully this book has provided you with some sound advice in these tough economic times. Though the current economic crisis we face will no doubt correct itself over time, we should also be aware of some of the long-term challenges of the federal debt, trade deficits, and unfunded liabilities. A wise financial steward will consider these looming threats as well.

The tough times we are experiencing provide a context for us to return to biblical principles of economics and finance. As Christians, we should model Christlike behavior. We should not be caught up in materialism and consumerism. We should be concerned with the poor and wary of the negative influence of wealth on our lives. We should be generous in our giving and thrifty in our spending. And we should make wise decisions about investments, inheritance, and insurance.

Seek out wise counsel (Proverbs 15:22) and advice. We are called to make the most of our money in tough times. This is an opportunity for all of us to model biblical principles before the watching world, while providing for ourselves and our families.

Notes

Chapter 1—Money

1. John Wesley, "The Use of Money," *The Sermons of John Wesley*, Thomas Jackson, ed., 1872 ed., http://wesley.nnu.edu/john_wesley/sermons/050.htm.

Chapter 2—Materialism and Consumerism

1. George Barna, *The Second Coming of the Church* (Nashville, TN: Word, 1998), 21.
2. John DeGraaf, David Wann, and Thomas Naylor, *Affluenza: The All-Consuming Epidemic*, 2nd ed. (San Francisco: Berrett-Koehler, 2005), xviii.
3. DeGraaf, Wann, and Naylor, 3.
4. U.S. Census Bureau, *Statistical Abstract of the United States* (Washington, DC: U.S. Government Printing Office, 2004–2005).
5. DeGraaf, Wann, and Naylor, 4.
6. DeGraaf, Wann, and Naylor, 42.
7. DeGraaf, Wann, and Naylor, 4.
8. Center for a New American Dream, 2004 survey, www.newdream.org/about/pdfs/Poll Release.pdf.
9. David Myers, *The American Paradox* (New Haven, CT: Yale University Press, 2000), 136.
10. Richard Swenson, *Margin: How to Create the Emotional, Physical, Financial, and Time Reserves You Need* (Colorado Springs, CO: NavPress, 1992).
11. Richard Swenson, *The Overload Syndrome: Learning to Live Within Your Limits* (Colorado Springs, CO: NavPress, 1998).
12. Kerby Anderson, *Signs of Warning, Signs of Hope* (Chicago, IL: Moody Press, 1994).
13. Alvin Toffler, *Future Shock* (New York: Bantam Books, 1971).
14. Bruce Horovitz, "You want it your way," *USA Today*, 3 April 2004, www.usatoday.com/money/industries/food/2004-03-04-picky_x.htm.
15. Swenson, *Overload Syndrome*, 86-87.
16. Swenson, *Overload Syndrome*, 46-47.
17. Swenson, as quoted in DeGraaf, Wann, and Naylor, 39.
18. James Kuntsler, in discussion with David Wann, March 1997, in DeGraaf, Wann, and Naylor, 65.
19. David Van Biema and Jeff Chu, "Does God Want You to Be Rich?" *Time*, 18 September 2006, www.time.com/time/magazine/article/0,9171,1533448,00.html.

Chapter 3—Giving

1. George Barna, "Tithing Down 62% in the Past Year," *Barna Update*, 19 May 2003, www.barna.org/FlexPage.aspx?Page=BarnaUpdate&BarnaUpdateID=139.

2. Quotes from Church Fathers from Randy Alcorn, *Money, Possessions and Eternity* (Wheaton, IL: Tyndale House Publishers, 2003), 185.

3. George Barna, "Evangelicals Are the Most Generous Givers, but Fewer than 10% of Born Again Christians Give 10% to Their Church," Barna Update, 5 April 2000, www.barna .org/FlexPage.aspx?Page=BarnaUpdate&BarnaUpdateID=52.

4. Barna, "Evangelicals."

Chapter 4—Debt and Credit

1. Bill Powell, "Life Without Credit," *Time*, 3 November 2008, 54.

2. The Holmes-Rahe Scale, www.geocities.com/beyond_stretched/holmes.htm.

3. National Postsecondary Student Aid Study, http://nces.ed.gov/surveys/npsas/.

4. Liz Pulliam Weston, "The big lie about credit card debt," MSN Money, 30 July 2007, http://articles.moneycentral.msn.com/Banking/CreditCardSmarts/TheBigLieAboutCred itCardDebt.aspx.

5. "How many credit cards is too many?" http://articles.moneycentral.msn.com/Banking/ CreditCardSmarts/HowManyCreditCardsIsTooMany.aspx; Robert Frank, *Luxury Fever* (New York: Free Press, 1999), 46.

6. Dun and Bradstreet, www.associatedcontent.com/article/142336/do_we_really_spend_ more_with_credit.html?cat=3.

7. M. Anderson, "Cash poor, choice rich, Paycheck-advance firms move in," *Sacramento Business Journal*, 11 January 1999.

8. Jane Bryant Quinn, "Payday Loans Can Be a Trap," *Newsweek*, 8 October 2007, 47.

Chapter 5—Saving and Investing

1. Barbara Dafoe Whitehead, "A Nation in Debt: How we killed thrift, enthroned loan sharks and undermined American prosperity," *The American Interest Online*, July/August 2008, www.the-american-interest.com/ai2/article.cfm?Id=458&MId=20.

2. David Tucker, *The Decline of Thrift in America* (New York: Praeger Publishers, 1990).

3. Consumer Federation of America, "More than half of Americans say they are not saving adequately," 10 December 2007, www.consumerfed.org/.

Chapter 7—Spending

1. Dave Ramsey, *The Total Money Makeover* (Nashville, TN: Thomas Nelson, 2007), 37.

2. Bill Powell, "Life Without Credit," *Time*, 3 November 2008, 58.

Chapter 8—The Bible and Economics

1. William Bradford, *Of Plymouth Plantation, 1620–1647*, ed. Samuel Eliot Morison (New York: Modern Library, 1967).

2. This list of governmental functions can be found in John Stapleford, *Bulls, Bears & Golden Calves* (Downers Grove, IL: InterVarsity Press, 2002), 86.

3. Adam Smith, *The Wealth of Nations*, book 4, chapter 2 (1776).

Chapter 9—Economic Questions

1. "America celebrates Tax Freedom Day," www.taxfoundation.org/publications/show/93 .html.

2. "Cost of Government Day," www.atr.org/national/cogd/index.html.
3. "Cost of Federal Regulation Grew to $1.16 Trillion," http://cei.org/node/20871.
4. "Ten Thousand Commandments: An Annual Snapshot of the Federal Regulatory State," http://cei.org/node/20871.
5. "States of Opportunity," *Wall Street Journal*, 12 February 2008, http://online.wsj.com/article/SB120277561232960623.html.
6. Laurence Kotlikoff, "Is the United States Bankrupt?" *Federal Reserve Bank of St. Louis Review*, July/August 2006, 88(4), pp. 235-249, research.stlouisfed.org/publications/review/06/07/Kotlikoff.pdf.
7. Laurence Kotlikoff, "Is the U.S. Going Broke?" *Forbes*, September 29, 2008, www.forbes.com/business/forbes/2008/0929/034.html.
8. Kotlikoff, "Is the U.S. Going Broke?"
9. Jagadeesh Gokhale and Kent Smetters, "Do the Markets Care About the $2.4 Trillion U.S. Deficit?" *Financial Analysts Journal*, March/April 2007.
10. Richard W. Fisher, "Storms on the Horizon," remarks before the Commonwealth Club of California (San Francisco, CA, May 28, 2008), www.dallasfed.org/news/speeches/fisher/2008/fs080528.cfm.
11. Fisher.
12. Raymond Moley, *After Seven Years* (New York: Harper & Brothers Publishers, 1939), 152.
13. Walter Williams, "Counterfeiting Versus Monetary Policy," 17 December 2008, http://townhall.com/columnists/WalterEWilliams/2008/12/17/counterfeiting_versus_monetary_policy.
14. John Maynard Keynes, *The Economic Consequences of Peace* (first published 1919; reprint 2007 by Skyhorse Publishing), 134, http://books.google.com/books?id=2ntLlfSf5bMC.
15. Keynes.
16. Shayne McGuire, *Buy Gold Now* (New York: John Wiley and Sons, 2008), 137.
17. Warren Buffett, "America's Growing Trade Deficit Is Selling the Nation Out From Under Us," *Fortune*, 26 October 2003, www.summitglobal.com/acrobat_pdf/warren_buffett_in_fortune_magazine_oct_03.pdf.
18. Thomas Friedman, *The World Is Flat: A Brief History of the Twenty-First Century* (New York: Farrar, Straus and Giroux, 2005), 9.
19. Friedman.
20. Friedman, 10.
21. Friedman, 49.
22. Friedman, 52.
23. Friedman, 123.
24. Friedman, 129.
25. Friedman, 237.

MORE BOOKS FROM KERBY ANDERSON

Current-issues expert Kerby Anderson provides well-informed, practical responses to topics you encounter every day. Backed by Scripture, scientific evidence, and the latest research, his approach equips Christians to bring a biblical perspective to today's important issues.

A Biblical Point of View on
Intelligent Design

"Have scientists been able to simulate evolution in the laboratory?" "What is the relationship between science and religion?" "What is the probability that the genetic code was formed by chance?" Voices on both sides of the evolution versus Intelligent Design debate say that science backs them up. But both cannot be right. Kerby Anderson examines the scientific evidence and asks the hard questions.

A Biblical Point of View on
Islam

"Do Christians and Muslims worship the same God?" "Is Islam a religion of peace?" "Does the Qur'an support the martyrdom of suicide bombers?" Even the world's top leaders and media organizations have helped spread inaccurate information, making it more difficult to understand Islam's teachings and followers. This concise guide reveals the misconceptions and addresses the crucial issues.

A Biblical Point of View on
Homosexuality

"Is a person born homosexual or is it a choice?" "Should same-sex marriages be legalized?" "What are some of the popular myths about homosexuality?" Balancing conviction with compassion and pointing to what the Bible really teaches on the subject, this guidebook brings into sharp focus the key issues and essential facts you need to know about homosexuality.

A Biblical Point of View on
Spiritual Warfare

"Is Satan for real, and how does he influence us?" "Can a believer be demon possessed?" "How can Christians keep from being spiritually deceived?" Kerby Anderson explores the Bible's guidelines for dealing with spiritual warfare, addressing common misconceptions and helping equip you to stand strong in the battles that come your way.

Other Harvest House resources to help you
with home management and stretching your dollar

The House That Cleans Itself
Creative Solutions for a Clean and Orderly House in Less Time Than You Can Imagine
Mindy Starns Clark

Have you wrestled with messiness and disorder for years? Are you looking for new ways to make housework easier? Here's great news! By adapting your house to fit your family's behavior, you can create a House That Cleans Itself.

Follow this step-by-step plan to discover...

- how to keep your house twice as clean in half the time
- how a stepladder, a camera, and a stopwatch will help you get started
- how to quickly change a messy area into a tidy one permanently
- how to anticipate and prevent messes before they happen
- how to get your family onboard in this new process

Plenty of creative suggestions, specific how-tos, and loads of encouragement help you and your family change your home from "messed" to "blessed" for good.

Working at Home
Lindsey O'Connor

A home-based business gives you the freedom to stay with the kids, be your own boss, and design a flexible work schedule—all without foregoing needed income or lifelong career goals. Home-business expert Lindsey O'Connor provides the inside information to help you reach your goals—

- ideas for starting a home business or bringing your current job home
- strategies for creating a marketing plan that works
- financial and tax aspects of running a home business
- ways to minister through your business
- hints for managing your time and avoiding procrastination

To read a sample chapter from these or other Harvest House books,
go to www.harvesthousepublishers.com

500 Time-Saving Hints for Every Woman
Helpful Tips for Your Home, Family, Shopping, and More
Emilie Barnes

In this easy-to-use resource, home-management expert Emilie Barnes reveals 500 fabulous secrets to creating a life that has less mess and more room for what really matters, helping you

- declutter your life and home
- stop piling it and start filing it
- begin each day with a to-do list
- clean efficiently and effectively
- tackle projects at home and elsewhere

Secrets to Getting More Done in Less Time
Donna Otto

Are you tired of clutter? Of being late? Of the endless struggle to get everything done? Home and life-management expert Donna Otto offers you easy-to-implement steps to getting your life in order. Whether you're disorganized or overworked, Donna's secrets to taking charge of your life will transform your harried schedule into one of efficiency and calm. You'll soon be able to...

- keep your house the way you want it to be
- use personalized planners effectively
- streamline shopping with check lists
- create joyful holiday gatherings
- involve the family so everybody benefits

Handy forms, time-proven advice, real-life examples, and contagious enthusiasm make Secrets to Getting More Done in Less Time productive and inspirational. Discover a lifestyle with room to breathe and celebrate!

To read a sample chapter from these or other Harvest House books,
go to www.harvesthousepublishers.com

Simple Secrets to a Beautiful Home
Creating a Place You and Your Family Will Love
Emilie Barnes

Aren't the best kinds of homemaking secrets the simple ones?

A beautiful home doesn't require too much money, too much energy, or too much time. Bestselling author and home-management expert Emilie Barnes shows you how you can easily weave beauty and happiness into the fabric of your daily life.

Simple Secrets to a Beautiful Home is an encouraging reminder that with just a touch of creativity, a splash of hospitality, and a sprinkle of welcome, you can simply enjoy, nurture, and transform your home.

*To read a sample chapter from these or other Harvest House books,
go to www.harvesthousepublishers.com*